THE SECRET AGENT and NOSTROMO

Christopher Hampton was born in the Azores in 1946. He wrote his first play, *When Did You Last See My Mother?* at the age of eighteen. His work for the theatre, television and cinema includes *The Philanthropist*, adaptations from Ibsen and Molière and the screenplays *Dangerous Liaisons* and *Carrington*.

Joseph Conrad (1857–1924) was born of Polish parents in the Ukraine. He enjoyed a seafaring life from 1874 to 1894 when he left the sea and devoted himself to literature. His best known works are *Lord Jim* (1900), *Heart of Darkness* (1902), *Nostromo* (1904), *The Secret Agent* (1907) and *Under Western Eyes* (1911).

by the same author

THE PHILANTHROPIST
TOTAL ECLIPSE
SAVAGES
TREATS
ABLE'S WILL: A PLAY FOR TELEVISION
TALES FROM HOLLYWOOD
LES LIAISONS DANGEREUSES
WHITE CHAMELEON

adaptations

George Steiner's THE PORTAGE TO SAN CHRISTOBAL OF A.H.
Lewis Carroll's ALICE'S ADVENTURES UNDER GROUND

screenplays

DANGEROUS LIAISONS
THE GINGER TREE
CARRINGTON
TOTAL ECLIPSE

translations

Odön von Horváth's TALES FROM THE VIENNA WOODS
Odön von Horváth's DON JUAN COMES BACK FROM THE WAR
Odön von Horváth's FAITH, HOPE AND CHARITY
Ibsen's THE WILD DUCK
Ibsen's HEDDA GABLER and A DOLL'S HOUSE
Molière's TARTUFFE

THE SECRET AGENT
and
NOSTROMO

Christopher Hampton

Based on the novels by
Joseph Conrad

faber and faber
LONDON · BOSTON

First published in 1996
by Faber and Faber Limited
3 Queen Square London WC1N 3AU

Photoset by Parker Typesetting Service, Leicester
Printed in England by Clays Ltd, St Ives plc

A CIP record for this book
is available from the British Library
ISBN 0-571-19026-X

2 4 6 8 10 9 7 5 3 1

For Norma
and Serge

CONTENTS

INTRODUCTION

In 1991, Bob Hoskins, no doubt tiring of the fact that Hollywood seemed only capable of seeing him either as cheeky chappie or thuggish heavy, decided he would like to direct a version of one of his favourite books, *The Secret Agent*, and invited the producer of his first American film (*The Honorary Consul*, which I had written), Norma Heyman, to work with him on it. They asked me to write it and I did. Everyone seemed happy with the script – among ourselves, I mean, since several potential investors reeled back, appalled at the darkness of the story. The only difficulty seemed to be that Bob could never find the necessary nine months to direct the film. Eventually, at the end of 1994, having unexpectedly enjoyed my own first attempt at directing (*Carrington*), I asked Bob if he would let me make the film. He agreed, apparently without hesitation. I had already dissuaded him from his original plan, which was to play the Professor, since, in my opinion, Verloc was a role he was born to play: and that was more or less that. There was some problem making the budget ($7 million) stretch, and eventually I traded a week's shooting for the money to build the principal set, exterior and interior, in Ealing Studios. Bob phoned Gérard Depardieu and Robin Williams and got them to agree to be in the film with what seemed like the greatest of ease. My first conversation with Gérard was his patient explanation of why, with his elaborate mass of commitments, he would regrettably be unable to be in the film after all: five minutes later, he called back and said: 'Ah, what the hell, I do it.'

It was a tougher film to make than *Carrington* for all sorts of reasons, not the least of which was that I had now learned enough to understand how little I knew. But I had a very good time all the same; and it confirmed my determination to persist with this second profession, which had come upon me so unpredictably and so late.

My Conrad years had begun, modestly enough, in the mid-eighties, when Stuart Burge proposed a television adaptation of

Nostromo. It had long been a source of puzzlement to me that what was then known as the BBC Classic Serial, though partial to Dickens and easily stirred to enthusiasm by one or other of the great female novelists of the nineteenth century, had given Joseph Conrad, despite his magnificently broad canvases, his virile plotting and his disturbing modernity, a wide berth; and so I eagerly agreed. *Nostromo*, like *Moby Dick*, is a book notoriously difficult to finish: indeed, to be honest, had I not chosen it as one of the two books I took with me on a boat trip to Rio (the other was Dostoevsky's *The Possessed*), I'm not sure I would have finished it myself, despite my unshakable admiration for Conrad. It seemed an ideal candidate for dramatization; and before long I had prepared a synopsis for a version in seven one-hour episodes.

It soon became clear that what Stuart and I envisaged was beyond the means of the BBC; and the quest for co-production financing began. I distinctly remember the moment, during a discussion with a South American TV executive, whose small feet were encased in dazzlingly shiny leather, about the availability or otherwise of the Venezuelan army, when it dawned on me that we hadn't a hope in hell: and so it proved.

A year or so later, I was summoned to see David Lean, whom I had met once before, sometime in the seventies, and liked, despite an alarmingly imperious manner, which, I later discovered, masked a sometimes painful shyness. After years of nomadic existence, spent mostly in hotel suites, he had bought two warehouses on a bend of the river at Limehouse, demolished one (except for its façade) to make a secluded garden and converted the other into a dauntingly sand-blasted palazzo with an elevator and a roof-terrace. His study, where we met, was on the ground floor; he sat at a wide desk with a plate-glass window and the river behind him. After a brief exchange of civilities, he clicked four Hermesetas into an immense yellow and cobalt blue Giverny teacup and fixed me across the desk with a magnetic glare. 'Nostromo,' he said and fell silent. 'Yes,' I prompted him; I was very excited. 'I gather you want to make a film of it.' I admitted that I did. 'So do I,' he said. 'Shall we do it? When are you free?' Fortunately, since I soon found out patience was not his strong suit, the answer was almost immediately.

The night before we were due to start working together, I was extremely anxious and slept fitfully; but just before dawn, I drifted off into what, sadly, has remained for me a unique experience: I dreamed the opening of the film. A fashionably dressed skeleton, silver ingots protruding from its frayed pockets, sits on the bottom of the sea. I tentatively put this to David, who seemed genuinely pleased with the image; also I managed to answer correctly (or, at least, not incorrectly) his potentially tricky question about which of his films I liked best (*Great Expectations*). So we seemed to have got off to a flying start; the process was under way.

It worked as follows: a taxi would arrive every morning at about nine to take me from Notting Hill to Limehouse. We would work for three hours or so and then go up to the top floor for a delicious lunch prepared by Sandra, David's companion, whom he subsequently married and who usually joined us. We were often accompanied by David's associate, Maggie Unsworth, who had worked with him on and off since his earliest films and who had, I believe, originally recommended me to David. I would resolve not to drink wine, but almost invariably weaken when it appeared. We'd go back to the study, where tea and cake would arrive at four, and the taxi would be called at about six, though I wouldn't necessarily leave until closer to seven. We certainly didn't work non-stop; David kept up a fascinating flow of anecdote and reminiscence, but every day we'd cover a considerable amount of ground.

Within a month or so we had worked out a quite detailed structure for the script, which was to remain more or less constant, despite the many vicissitudes to come: and I withdrew to write, while David and Sandra set off on an epic journey, involving the Concorde, the QEII and the Warner Bros. private jet, to inspect a site on the Gulf of California, on the inside of the finger of Baja in Mexico, which had been proposed by our designer John Box as the ideal location for the port of Sulaco and the tranquil, unruffled waters of the Golfo Placido. The first draft took me about six weeks, by which time David was back and extremely impatient; it was all I could do to persuade him to let me finish before I showed him what I'd written. And as soon as he'd read it, the year of the rewrite began.

It wasn't so much that David disliked sections of the script; as I've said, its basic form was to remain intact: it was more that his restless perfectionism would never allow him to concede that we might have arrived at any sort of final solution. This was especially true of the sequences closest to his heart, the action montages: the opening section; the ball given by the Goulds to keep up morale as the Civil War takes a disastrous turn; the riot in the town (which he called 'the day of dust'); the bringing down of the silver consignment from the mine to the harbour; the famous escape by boat across the pitch-black waters of the Golfo Placido; and Nostromo's epic journey over the mountains to bring back General Barrios and his new repeating rifles. These sequences were raked over and over to find the most effective cuts and the most fluid dramatic narrative. David judged everything with an editor's ruthless eye and called in the most detailed kind of assistance to help us towards a decision. Thus, the storyboard artist would be asked to provide three small water-colours, so that we could judge whether a certain moment might best be served by a cut or a dissolve. One day, John Alcott, the prospective director of photography, who was to die suddenly later in the year, joined a fascinating discussion on how the central sequence – the escape by boat, which, for plot reasons, has to take place in total darkness – was to be lit. I had found, in my researches, a nineteenth-century travel book which described the unusually bright phosphorescence in Venezuelan coastal waters; John spoke of using the star-filled skies of southern latitudes and of silhouettes and pencil-lights; and David came up with the unrealistic but extraordinarily imaginative idea of making the silver itself, the film's true central character, a light source. Slowly, I began to understand why David had a reputation of being uncomfortable with actors: everything was so meticulously pre-imagined down to the composition of each frame, that actors, with their messy human presence, their unpredictable impulses and, worst of all, their independent ideas and suggestions were inevitably destabilizing elements. Some, like Katharine Hepburn or Charles Laughton, Celia

Johnson or Claude Rains were able to circumvent this difficulty in some miraculous way and give him exactly what he had in mind, and they retained his undying loyalty; while others, like Alec Guinness or Trevor Howard, who served him no less well, evidently had a tendency to confuse him by offering dissenting opinions and possibilities he had not envisaged; and occasionally he would come across an actor who would fight him every inch of the way, like Judy Davis in *A Passage to India*, of whom, paradoxically, he always spoke with a kind of baffled affection. On the other hand, he relied on and was fond of writers and often referred warmly to H. E. Bates, Terence Rattigan or Noël Coward, with whom he had made his first four films; and for me, the first six months was an education in narrative film technique and structural rigour.

Six months had in fact been the amount of time I had, with foolish optimism, set aside for the completion of the *Nostromo* screenplay. But it was longer than that before David pronounced himself grudgingly satisfied with the first draft and set off to discuss it with the producer, Steven Spielberg. He returned from Los Angeles in an extremely bad mood: not only had Steven presumed to give him some notes on the script (later, when I came across them, they seemed eminently sensible), but the studio, Warners, had indicated that they would like to minimize their risk by putting up only half the (extravagantly large) budget and raising the rest of the financing elsewhere. This *lèse-majesté* had decided David to take his trade elsewhere; and to return with redoubled vigour to those aspects of the screenplay he still found troubling.

Despite the boldness of his imagery (a word which, like the word 'artist', he found unacceptably pretentious), he remained timid about an audience's ability to deal with any other kind of complexity. To initiate any kind of a discussion about capitalism, say, or colonialism was out of the question. In my view, David had been confused by the overwhelming success of one of his least good films, *Dr Zhivago*, which had encouraged him to believe in the efficacy of certain forms of over-simplification. Consequently, he had the greatest difficulty with the character of Martin Decoud, the dilettante writer and Hamlet figure of the novel, who is destroyed by the silver of the

San Tomé mine as remorselessly as Gould, the entrepreneur and man of action, and Nostromo, the man of the people. David detested intellectuals as a breed; he thought them snobbish, condescending, dishonest and impotent. His instinct was therefore to ridicule or caricature Decoud. He wouldn't accept that if the architecture of the novel proposed the destruction of three completely different types of men by the same malign force, the three men in question should be given if not the same weight, at least the same sympathy. So a great many of our discussions hinged around my defence of this character, whom David wanted to be able to listen to less and dislike more.

A more surprising problem was David's objection to the character of Hirsch, the German-Jewish small businessman whose cowardice and panic lead to his fortuitous presence on board the silver-carrying lighter in the Golfo Placido and to his eventual torture and death. I couldn't understand this, until David eventually explained the source of his unease: the accusations of anti-Semitism in the portrayal of Fagin in *Oliver Twist* (a masterpiece, to my mind), which had prevented the film's release in America for over a year and ensured it a rocky reception when it eventually came out. I pointed out that Hirsch redeems himself with a final courageous gesture, that his presence on the boat is essential to build up the tension in what is perhaps the most memorable sequence in the film, and that the crucified corpse of Hirsch (subject of one of John Box's most telling drawings for the film) presiding over Nostromo's long conversation with Dr Monygham is the crucial factor in Nostromo's decision to go on helping Gould and the ruling élite: but it was a subject that nagged at David like a toothache and he continued to circle around it.

And so the months rolled by, I struggling to find new solutions to what were by now old problems or to defend more eloquently some strongly-held position under renewed attack, while behind David's large head, through the plate-glass window, a French destroyer, with all its crew lined up on deck saluting, would sail distractingly by. In the depths of winter, David and Sandra moved to the Marbella Club where, for several weeks, I would spend Tuesday to Friday working with David perhaps at an even more intensive rate than usual (one day, Sandra put her head round the door and pointed out that we hadn't left the room for more than twelve hours). It was there we felt we had finally solved the difficult, long encounter of Nostromo and Dr Monygham at the Customs House: so some progress was still being made.

By now, I had accumulated over a thousand pages of manuscript; and I had begun to formulate a distressing theory: namely, that for some reason David was more interested in continuing to work on the screenplay than in actually making the film. This was fine for the first nine months or so when, in my opinion, the script continued to improve, but now we seemed to be going round in circles. And I had a more pressing problem: if I didn't write my screenplay of *Dangerous Liaisons* in more or less record time, the project seemed likely to be abandoned in the face of Milos Forman's rival, bigger-budget, altogether more heavyweight version. So I gave a month's notice. David took it in a dignified fashion, but there was no avoiding the fact that his feelings were hurt. I promised to do as much as I could in the coming month and return at the end of the year when my other script would be finished. We worked until eleven o'clock on the Saturday evening of the final week; and when I left, his manner was gruff.

In fact, I wrote the *Liaisons* script in three weeks, but I was also co-producing the film and looking for a director, so it occupied a good deal more than the writing time. I kept in close touch with David until one day when I called him on a weekend from the Joinville Studio in Paris. He seemed distracted, so I asked him if anything was the matter. 'No,' he said, 'as a matter of fact I'm here with Robert.' I knew immediately what he meant. Robert was Robert Bolt, with whom after years of estrangement, I'd engineered a reconciliation; and what was meant was that David's patience was at an end.

After this, I saw him very rarely: he was as stringent an editor in life as he was in the cutting-room. He and Robert worked on for another three years, eliminating the character of Hirsch and turning Decoud into a dandified French fop (I had never been able to persuade David that Decoud, despite his name, was not a Frenchman, but a Costaguanan in exile in Paris). Finally, David did a last draft on his own: I read it recently. It was so concentrated an essence, so abstract a succession of vividly imagined tableaux, that he must at some point have stopped worrying about how much the audience would understand. He had found a new studio, Tri-Star, a new producer who had nothing whatsoever in common with his predecessor except for his initials, Serge Silberman, and had made the decision to shoot not in Central or South America but in his old hunting ground, Spain, and the Victorine Studio in Nice. The budget ($45 million) was raised, the sets were built, a cast had been assembled and a stand-by director had been appointed in case of David's illness or incapacity. But he was already ill, with a frighteningly fast-moving cancer; and six weeks before shooting was due to start, he died. I shall always be sorry not to have seen the film he would have made.

David Lean's death left *Nostromo* in a tangled situation: as I understand it, all relevant material passed into the possession of an insurance company. Serge Silberman waited for eighteen months or so and then made an offer for what, to the insurance company, was merely a useless paper mountain. Taking delivery of the heap, he was surprised to discover among it my script, the existence of which David had never mentioned to him. He liked it, contacted me, and so it was that a new friendship began with a man who had produced some of my favourite films, from Buñuel's last French pictures to Kurosawa's *Ran*. Over the first of a long series of gourmet meals in Paris, Serge asked me who I thought should direct the film: and I told him that the younger director David had felt closest to was Hugh Hudson.

And so a new phase began, and in 1993 I was able to feed in everything I'd learned from David and at the same time write exactly the script I'd had in mind in the first place. The most liberating, simplifying stroke for me was to remove the character of Captain Mitchell, the kindly but self-important harbour master, who acts as a kind of occasional narrator in the novel, but never seemed to have much of a function in the film; while the suggestion that Nostromo, in his domestic scenes with the Viola family, should speak Italian (David had an instinctive horror of subtitles) seemed a useful way to distinguish him both from the Anglo-Saxon and the South American communities.

When the script was done, we all set off for Mexico, first to Alamos, an almost untouched colonial town in Sonora, and then to Loreto, John Box's discovery, which David and Sandra had visited back in 1986. We calculated that with judicious effort we could knock at least a third off David's budget: and there, to this day, the matter has rested. Hollywood has always been a spawning-ground of paradox, but in its current climate there seems little likelihood that anyone will be tempted to invest $30 million in a story whose essential point is that money is the root of all evil.

Christopher Hampton

THE SECRET AGENT

The Secret Agent opened in the US in November 1996. The cast and crew includes:

VERLOC	Bob Hoskins
WINNIE	Patricia Arquette
OSSIPON	Gérard Depardieu
CHIEF INSPECTOR HEAT	Jim Broadbent
STEVIE	Christian Bale
VLADIMIR	Eddie Izzard
WINNIE'S MOTHER	Elizabeth Spriggs
THE DRIVER	Peter Vaughan
THE ASSISTANT COMMISSIONER	Julian Wadham
MICHAELIS	Roger Hammond
YUNDT	Ralph Nossek
TICKET CLERK	Neville Phillips

Director/Writer	Christopher Hampton
Producer	Norma Heyman
Executive Producer	Bob Hoskins
Director of Photography	Denis Lenoir AFC
Production Designer	Caroline Amies
Film Editor	George Akers
Costume Designer	Anushia Nieradzik
Music by	Philip Glass

EXT. BRETT STREET IN SOHO. EVENING

The camera accompanies, at about waist-height, an as yet unidentified figure in frayed overcoat and disintegrating shoes, moving with unnatural deliberation through the dingy streets of Soho in the year 1886. It's still only late afternoon, but the winter darkness is penetrated only by the orange glow from the low shop-fronts and the bluish radiance of the street-lamps, lending the mud and slime of pavement and cobbles a viscous sheen. The streets are still relatively crowded with vehicles and bustling pedestrians, many of whom are held up by the funereal pace maintained by our man, who now turns a corner into a quieter street. As he does so, an urchin hurries up with hand outstretched, begging by reflex; until he catches sight of his client, at which point he withdraws his hand as if it's been scalded and slinks away.

ANOTHER ANGLE *explains why: at first glance, the shabby figure of the* PROFESSOR, *with his thin hair and protruding ears, looks harmless enough, but behind his round, black-rimmed spectacles, his ice-cold eyes gleam with such ferocity and his lip curls with such contempt as to strike fear into the heart of the boldest begger. As the urchin scurries off, the* PROFESSOR *permits himself a wintry spark of amusement: then he moves on, slow but assured.*

As the crowds thin out and disappear, the PROFESSOR *comes to a halt in front of a seedy, deserted, ill-lit shop, beneath a yellow, unconvincing sign which says 'Books'. The shop forms part of the ground floor of a tall, narrow, brick house. Lamps are lit upstairs on the first floor and in the front room on the second floor as well.*

The PROFESSOR *leans forward to look through one of the small, grimy window-panes of the shop; and the camera, following his* POV, *ranges over: copies of yellowing newspapers (the* Torch, *the* Gong, *the* Anarchist); *brown envelopes and parcels marked 2/6 or 3/-; some French magazines hanging across a string; and finally some packets of photographs of dancing girls or rather beefy naked women lashed to pillars.*

The PROFESSOR *straightens up and a sardonic amusement once again plays across his features. He seems about to step through the half-open shop door, when a burst of raised voices comes from the room above the shop front, stopping him in his tracks. He takes a step back and his face comes up, caught in the lamplight, suddenly contorted with a strange hatred. Automatically, his hand goes to to the left-hand pocket of his shiny jacket. He stands there for a moment, his face a mask of pure rage; then turns and moves abruptly out of frame.*

Once he's gone, the camera begins to move up the façade of the building, past the 'Books' sign, to look in the first-floor windows at a smoke-filled room where some kind of meeting is in progress, no doubt, to judge from the extravagance of the gestures and the intemperance of the sound-level, a political meeting. But the camera travels past this to the floor above, through the window and across a dark, empty room and landing into a second room, where a young woman moves to and fro, putting clothes into an open suitcase, watched by a standing younger man with a strangely vacant stare and an older woman, who is dabbing at her eyes with a lace handkerchief.

INT. SPARE BEDROOM IN VERLOC'S HOUSE. EVENING

The young woman, WINNIE VERLOC, *is striking-looking and gives an immediate impression of maturity beyond her years (she's in her mid- to late twenties). There's something grave and enigmatic in her expression, even when, as now, exasperation is quite close to the surface. Her* MOTHER, *a disorganized-looking woman in her fifties, adjusting an ill-fitting auburn wig and wearing an ancient silk dress, festooned with yellowing cotton lace, is evidently in awe of her; while her brother* STEVIE, *a slight seventeen-year-old with a drooping lower lip, a tendency to stammer when excited and a mental age of roughly half his actual age, is entirely devoted to her, a devotion which, however much* WINNIE *may find it necessary to scold or correct him, is completely mutual.*

WINNIE *tries, unsuccessfully at first, to close the bulging suitcase, an ancient cardboard affair with a minimum of flexibility.*

WINNIE: I still can't understand what it is we done wrong, Mother.

MOTHER: Oh, no, dear, it's nothing like that, really, it's . . . (*She breaks off, on the verge of tears, but* WINNIE *is in no mood to let her off the hook.*)

WINNIE: Weren't you comfortable enough here, was that it?

(WINNIE*'s* MOTHER *shakes her head, speechless before the enormity of this suggestion. Eventually, as* WINNIE *succeeds in closing the reluctant suitcase, she's sufficiently composed to venture a* non-sequitur.)

MOTHER: I purposely left you my few bits of good furniture. I don't see the use of waiting till I'm dead.

(WINNIE *looks up at her sharply; then across at* STEVIE.)

WINNIE: Stevie.

STEVIE: Yes, Winnie.

WINNIE: You go and do some of your drawing. I'll call you when it's time to bring the luggage down.

STEVIE: All right, Winnie.

(*He smiles at her and leaves the room meekly.*)

INT. MAIN BEDROOM IN VERLOC'S HOUSE. EVENING

STEVIE *crosses the landing and steps into the darkened front bedroom, where he opens the third drawer of a substantial chest of drawers. It's full of his possessions: a coloured ball, a clown doll, a frayed bear, once musical, which tinkles as he moves it. There are also a number of pieces of paper covered in perfect circles, which he moves aside to get at a pencil and a pad of plain paper. He's close enough to hear the women talking behind him, but doesn't react in any way.*

WINNIE: (*Off-screen*) What you want to say that for in front of him, you know how upset he gets if anyone talks about dying.

MOTHER: (*Off-screen*) I'm sorry, dear, I wasn't thinking . . .

INT. STAIRCASE. EVENING

STEVIE *sets off down the stairs, and the debate raging below begins to drown out the voices of his mother and sister. He has a moment of confusion, not wanting to go down and interrupt the proceedings, when a happy inspiration strikes him and he simply sits down on the stairs, where only the lower half of his body is lit, opens his pad and begins, with great skill and concentration, to draw more perfect circles, of different sizes, but all uncannily accurate. From the room below, an even voice rises, wheezing but authoritative: the voice of the paroled revolutionary,* MICHAELIS, *speaking its precise but accented English.*

MICHAELIS: (*Off-screen*) A revolution cannot be provoked: it must arise spontaneously by the will of the people at the moment when it becomes clear to them that capitalism is ready to collapse under the weight of its own contradictions.

INT. SITTING-ROOM. EVENING

During this, the camera tracks down into the room where the meeting is taking place. There are a dozen or so participants, mostly men, although there are two or three women present, including an extraordinary, ancient crone who is literally sitting at the feet of one of the four men who are to have most claim on our attention: KARL YUNDT, *a scrawny old German of melodramatic appearance, with a white goatee, a broad-brimmed hat and a shabby green havelock. The speaker,* MICHAELIS, *is, by contrast, respectable in a grey suit, although his extreme pallor and obesity make him an equally remarkable figure. Comrade* ALEXANDER OSSIPON *is a younger man, a big, blond Russian with shrewd blue eyes and a home-made cigarette-holder. Finally, the owner of the premises,* ADOLF VERLOC, *a bulky man with the air of having spent the day wallowing in an unmade bed in his crumpled clothes, perched on the sofa, his eyes now glazed with boredom, at other times registering, by no means sympathetically, the arguments of his companions.*

YUNDT, *ensconced in a large horsehair armchair by the fire, swivels round to counter-attack* MICHAELIS.

YUNDT: Have you still not understood that your damned pessimism is a way of lying down and allowing the oppressor to march all over you?

MICHAELIS: Pessimism! If I were a pessimist, don't you think that sometime in that fifteen years I would have found a way to cut my throat?

INT. STAIRCASE. EVENING

STEVIE, *hearing this, looks up from his drawing. His lower lip begins to tremble.*

MICHAELIS: (*Off-screen*) At the very least, I could have beaten my head in against the walls of my cell.

INT. SITTING-ROOM. EVENING

MICHAELIS *wheezes, partially strangled by his own vehemence.*

MICHAELIS: No, I am not advising resignation or indifference: I am counselling patience!

OSSIPON: Patience: another word for doing nothing. You are saying that all action is useless.

YUNDT: Worse than that. You are offering encouragement to those economic cannibals who drink the blood and feed on the flesh of the people.

VERLOC: Hear, hear!

INT. STAIRCASE. EVENING

STEVIE *stares ahead of him, rigid with terror, suppressing a sob.*

MICHAELIS: (*Off-screen*) No, no, patience is not submission, it is a state of mind in which to complete the necessary preparations for the future.

INT. SITTING-ROOM. EVENING

YUNDT *leans forward, spittle spraying from between his irregular teeth, as he pounds a big thick stick on the floor for emphasis.*

YUNDT: If I could find three men, three, capable of feeling no pity for anything on earth, including themselves, then I could make the necessary preparations for the future.

MICHAELIS: You cannot force what must happen of its own accord. Before long, the property-owners will begin to fight among themselves.

INT. STAIRCASE. EVENING

YUNDT: (*Off-screen*) And in the meantime, they hold their branding-irons against the skin of the people and we must hear it sizzle . . .

(*At this,* STEVIE *breaks down and begins to blubber noisily.*)

INT. SITTING-ROOM. EVENING

YUNDT: . . . and make no response, except for your damned patience, to the smell of burning . . .

(*He has faltered at the sound of* STEVIE*'s sobbing; and now breaks off: all the participants in the debate look up and a silence falls, as a piece of white paper floats slowly through the* *currents of rising air to land on the floor.* OSSIPON *is the first to react, crossing the room to gather up the piece of paper; and* VERLOC *rises to his feet, alarmed.*)

INT. STAIRCASE. EVENING

STEVIE *sobs, his fists clenched and his eyes closed tight.* WINNIE *arrives in a flurry; she's wearing her hat and coat.*

WINNIE: Stevie: whatever's the matter?

STEVIE: B-b-b-branding-irons. Must hurt, Winnie; think how it must hurt.

WINNIE: Never mind that, the cab's here. It's time to help mother down with her luggage.

STEVIE: But it's got to be stopped, Winnie.

(WINNIE *reaches down and takes hold of his hand, her tone tender.*)

WINNIE: Come along, don't you worry about it. Mr Verloc will stop it.

(*By now,* VERLOC *has reached the bottom of the stairs; he looks up at them in some annoyance.*)

VERLOC: We're trying to conduct a meeting down here. Stop that fuss.

STEVIE: I'm sorry, Mr Verloc.

WINNIE: We're just leaving.

(STEVIE *is on his feet now, his expression sheepish. He allows himself to be led away by* WINNIE.)

INT. SITTING-ROOM. EVENING

VERLOC *plods back across the room, frowning.*

VERLOC: I'm sorry about this, gentlemen, we may as well take a pause. My mother-in-law is moving out this evening.

(*He's on his way back to his corner of the sofa, when* OSSIPON *intercepts him, flourishing the piece of paper.*)

OSSIPON: It's very good, this. Absolutely typical.

VERLOC: What's very good?

(OSSIPON *shows him.*)

(INSET: *the piece of paper, covered with innumerable perfect circles.*)

OSSIPON: Exactly what you would expect from a degenerate.

VERLOC: I wouldn't let my wife hear you call him that, if I were you. She's very fond of her brother.
OSSIPON: It's a purely scientific term.

(STEVIE *comes clumping down the stairs, carrying two suitcases. He's followed by his* MOTHER, *who wears a cloak and a black and mauve bonnet; and by* WINNIE, *who carries a smaller suitcase.*

STEVIE *stumbles and almost falls; but he recovers himself, moves across the half-landing, not looking to right or left and continues down the stairs. At the appearance of the ladies, only* MICHAELIS *heaves himself to his feet and moves forward to shake hands with* WINNIE, *with a courtly bow.*)

WINNIE: Mr Michaelis.
MICHAELIS: Mrs Verloc.

(WINNIE *shoots a far from friendly glance at* YUNDT, *who looks back at her, his expression truculent. Meanwhile* OSSIPON *has arrived at* WINNIE*'s side and is attempting to take the suitcase from her.*)

OSSIPON: Please, allow me, Mrs Verloc.
WINNIE: I can manage, Mr Ossipon.
OSSIPON: Please, call me Tom.
WINNIE: I thought your name was Alexander.
OSSIPON: It is: but all my most special friends call me Tom.

(*He's succeeded, during this, in wresting her suitcase away from her, brushing his hand against hers as he does so. She looks away, blushing somewhat, but aware that he's continuing to stare at her quite shamelessly.*)

EXT. SHOP FRONT. BRETT STREET. EVENING

A decrepit hackney carriage waits by the muddy kerb. The DRIVER, *slumped on the box, waits in an attitude of dejection behind his bony and emaciated horse.* STEVIE *emerges from the shop, puts the suitcases down on the pavement and grins up at the* DRIVER, *who contemplates him stonily.*

INT. SHOP. EVENING

VERLOC *and his* MOTHER-IN-LAW *move across the strange, indirectly-lit body of the shop, followed by* OSSIPON *and* WINNIE. *The party comes to a halt as* VERLOC *hands* WINNIE*'s sniffling*

MOTHER *his large white pocket handkerchief.*

VERLOC: You can come back any time you wish, you know that.

MOTHER: Oh, Mr Verloc, you're so kind.

EXT. SHOP FRONT. EVENING

The DRIVER *stares down at* STEVIE, *then speaks in a hoarse, strained whisper.*

DRIVER: Lissen, do me a favour, will yer, young feller, load the bags for me, I'm not supposed to do no lifting.

(*He flourishes his left arm, previously unseen; it ends in a primitive metal hook.* STEVIE, *once he's got over his shock, stares up at this with unabashed fascination.*)

Well, go on then.

(STEVIE *snaps out of it, begins loading the bags.*)

INT. SHOP. EVENING

As VERLOC *and his* MOTHER-IN-LAW *pass out of the shop,* OSSIPON *leans towards* WINNIE, *his expression concerned.*

OSSIPON: Is he all right, your brother?

(*He hands her back* STEVIE*'s drawing.*)

WINNIE: He's a little upset today.

OSSIPON: Upset?

(*They pass on, out of the shop.*)

EXT. SHOP FRONT. EVENING

STEVIE *is loading the bags.* WINNIE*'s* MOTHER *is in tears.*

MOTHER: I'm ever so grateful, Mr Verloc.

VERLOC: Not at all.

WINNIE: Tell her, Adolf, nobody wanted her to move out.

VERLOC: What? Oh. No. Course not.

(*He opens the door of the cab, anxious to be rid of them. Between them, he and* WINNIE *manage to bundle her* MOTHER *in and* WINNIE *speaks to him under her breath.*)

WINNIE: I won't be long.

VERLOC: I'll get rid of them, soon as I can.

(WINNIE *steps into the cab, indicating to* STEVIE *that he should climb up on to the box with the* DRIVER.)

INT. CAB. EVENING

WINNIE'S MOTHER *is sobbing helplessly. She tries to control herself, as* OSSIPON *leans into the cab to stow the remaining suitcase. This done, he leers up at* WINNIE.

OSSIPON: Safe journey.

(*She looks at him, her expression slightly alarmed, not responding to his charmingly crooked smile.*)

EXT. BRETT STREET. EVENING

OSSIPON *seems disposed to wait, but* VERLOC, *who's already turned away, turns back and tugs at his sleeve.*

VERLOC: Come on, we should get back.

(OSSIPON *follows, reluctantly.*

Up on the box, the DRIVER *has wrapped the reins around his hook. Now, with his good hand, he reaches for the whip.*)

STEVIE: Don't.

DRIVER: Eh?

STEVIE: Don't whip.

DRIVER: Oh.

STEVIE: You mustn't whip. It hurts.

DRIVER: Mustn't whip, eh?

(*And so saying, he brings the whip down in a savage cut across the horse's flanks. The horse, galvanized, begins to strain: but nothing happens.*

The DRIVER *lashes again; and a third time: and finally the wheel drags out of the mud and the cab begins to move.*

CLOSE *on* STEVIE: *he's tormented by horror and compassion.*)

INT. CAB. NIGHT

WINNIE *and her* MOTHER *are bounced and jolted as the cab rattles along. After a while,* WINNIE *reacts with impatience when her* MOTHER *is unable to restrain a choking series of sobs.*

WINNIE: This was all your idea, Mother, so I don't know why you're carrying on.

MOTHER: I can't help it, dear, I'm sorry.

WINNIE: You haven't quarrelled with Mr Verloc, have you?

MOTHER: Course not. Mr Verloc has always been the soul of generosity.

WINNIE: Then whatever is it decided you to leave us?

(*Her* MOTHER *looks away, reluctant to answer. Eventually, she turns back to* WINNIE.)

MOTHER: I never could get used to that shop. I had to keep me eyes shut every time I passed through. Wasn't the sort of place you could very well ask someone back for a cup of tea, now was it?

WINNIE: It's a steady business.

MOTHER: I don't know what your dad would have said.

WINNIE: Dad was a brute.

MOTHER: Winnie!

WINNIE: Well, he was: he used to take it out on Stevie something terrible.

MOTHER: Stevie was a disappointment to him.

EXT. CAB. NIGHT

STEVIE*'s staring, open-mouthed, at something which has caught his attention.*

MOTHER: (*Voice-over*) He couldn't get used to the idea of having a boy who was a bit, well, not quite right in the head.

(*It's the hook which is fascinating* STEVIE. *He begins to reach out towards it.*)

WINNIE: (*Voice-over*) Taking his belt off to him wasn't going to make him any cleverer, was it?

(STEVIE *can't resist touching the hook: he does so and the* DRIVER, *noticing, pushes him away.*)

EXT. STREET. NIGHT

LONG SHOT *of the cab as it rounds a corner past some derelict buildings. The* DRIVER *cracks his whip. Suddenly, quite unexpectedly,* STEVIE *rises to his feet and leaps from the moving carriage.*

INT. CAB. NIGHT

WINNIE *gasps in shock as* STEVIE*'s body whistles past the window.*

EXT. STREET. NIGHT

The cab lurches to a halt as STEVIE *rises from the ground and begins to wipe the dirt off his palms with his ever-present white handkerchief.* WINNIE *bursts from the cab, as her* MOTHER *wails ineffectually in the background.*

MOTHER: Oh, my Lord, now what? Is the boy hurt, is he hurt?

(WINNIE, *indignant, grabs* STEVIE *by the sleeve. He's holding his hands out to ward her off.*)

STEVIE: It's all right, Winnie, it's all right.

WINNIE: You get back up this minute!

STEVIE: No, walk, Winnie, I'll walk. I'll run after.

WINNIE: What are you talking about?

STEVIE: It's too heavy, Winnie. For the horse.

WINNIE: Run after a cab, I've never heard of such a thing!

(*There's a muffled cry from* WINNIE*'s* MOTHER, *inside the cab.*)

MOTHER: Don't you let him, Winnie, he'll get lost!

WINNIE: I'll tell Mr Verloc, Stevie, he'll be ever so unhappy.

(STEVIE *looks at her for a moment, his face working. Then, without another word, he climbs back up on to the box; and* WINNIE *gets back into the cab.*)

EXT. BOX OF THE CAB AND STREETS. EVENING

The DRIVER *watches* STEVIE *as he clambers back up; his croaking voice is thick with righteous indignation.*

DRIVER: You been drinking?

(STEVIE*'s expression is so blankly ingenuous that the* DRIVER *is disarmed.*)

Well, don't you go for trying that again.

(*He brings the whip down hard and the horse strains and heaves to restart the cab.*)

STEVIE: Poor horse.

DRIVER: Nemmine the 'orse. 'Ow'd you like to sit up 'ere, two o'clock in the morning?

(*He emphasizes the point by striking* STEVIE *in the chest with his hook.* STEVIE *looks back at him, wide-eyed with appalled compassion.*)

See, I'm a night cabby. I got to take what they bloody well give me. Picking up all sorts, middle of the night. Wife and four kids to keep.

(*He lashes the horse again: by now the cab is rattling along.*)

'S a 'ard world.

STEVIE: Bad. Very bad.

DRIVER: 'Ard on 'orses: but a damn' sight 'arder on poor bleeders like me.

(STEVIE*'s eyes are bright with tears.*)

STEVIE: You can come in my bed if you like.

(*The* DRIVER *shoots a startled glance at him.*)

And your horse as well. I'll ask Winnie.

(*The* DRIVER *doesn't answer; instead, he edges away from* STEVIE.)

INT. CAB. NIGHT

WINNIE*'s* MOTHER *looks shrewdly across at* WINNIE.

MOTHER: I'm doing this for Stevie. To make sure he'll be safe. Same reason you married Mr Verloc, if the truth be known.

WINNIE: What do you mean?

MOTHER: Don't tell me you didn't prefer that butcher's boy, Ron. Nice-looking boy, liked a laugh. But you wanted someone who'd be able to look after Stevie.

WINNIE: Mr Verloc's always liked Stevie.

MOTHER: Yes, but he can sometimes be a burden: and now I'm getting on a bit, I was afraid I might be as well.

WINNIE: No . . .

MOTHER: Even the best of men can get tired. I didn't want him to get tired of Stevie.

WINNIE: He'd have to get tired of me first.

(*She's spoken with great determination and finality: now she turns away to look out of the window.*)

EXT. STREET. NIGHT

The cab trundles on, the horse heaving it down the street, egged on by the whip and the cries of the DRIVER.

EXT. ALMSHOUSES. NIGHT

The luggage has been stowed away, the cab has vanished and now WINNIE *and* STEVIE *say goodbye to their* MOTHER *in the deserted forecourt of the row of almshouses, tiny gabled cottages looking on to a gravel drive encircling a patch of muddy lawn.* WINNIE*'s* MOTHER *is making an heroic, but not entirely successful effort to hold back her tears.*

MOTHER: You'll come and see me, won't you, Winnie, often as you can?

WINNIE: Course I will.

(STEVIE *submits passively to his* MOTHER*'s embrace; she speaks over his shoulder to* WINNIE.)

MOTHER: I want to see you every Sunday.

WINNIE: I'll come when I can manage: and when I can't, I'll send you Stevie.

MOTHER: Not on his own, dear, you have to change buses, he'll get lost.

WINNIE: You leave it to me, I'll work out something.

(*There is a dangerous silence as* STEVIE *is released by his* MOTHER*;* WINNIE *acts briskly to defuse the situation, as* STEVIE *looks up at a distant clap of thunder. It's beginning to rain.*)

You'd better go in, mother, you'll catch cold out here.

(STEVIE*'s lip is quivering and* WINNIE *turns her attention to him.*)

And you look after me on the way home, help me into the bus.

(*This does the trick:* STEVIE*'s expression clears.*)

STEVIE: Mustn't be nervous, Winnie. I'll look after you.

(WINNIE*'s* MOTHER *half-smiles, reassured by this exchange, and abruptly turns away.*)

EXT. STREET. NIGHT

STEVIE, *arm-in-arm with* WINNIE *and holding on tight, steers her along the pavement of a wide but squalid East End street, moving from one pool of sickly gaslight to another. By now, it's pouring with rain.*

STEVIE: It's a hard world, Winnie.

WINNIE: That's true enough.

STEVIE: Hard on horses. And for poor people.

WINNIE: Nobody can do anything about that, Stevie.

STEVIE: Yes. Police.

(WINNIE *lets out a snort of laughter.*)

WINNIE: That's not what the police are there for.

(STEVIE *frowns. They walk on until they reach the bus-stop and come to a halt beneath it.* STEVIE*'s expression is still troubled.*)

STEVIE: Then what are they there for, Winnie?

WINNIE: The police are there so's them as have nothing can't take nothing away from them as have a lot.

(*He accepts some coins for the bus fare, but he's still grappling with the implications of this: then he bursts into tears.*)

STEVIE: What can they do, Winnie, if they're poor and hungry?

(WINNIE *takes him in her arms and hugs him fiercely.*)

WINNIE: You mustn't worry about it, Stevie: things don't stand much looking into.

(STEVIE *hangs on to her, sobbing helplessly.*)

Long as you and me love each other, Stevie, that's the important thing.

(*A horse-drawn bus trundles laboriously around the corner. Distracted by this,* STEVIE *stops crying, quite suddenly. Then he remembers what he was going to say.*)

STEVIE: Mr Verloc: does he love me?

WINNIE: Of course he does, Stevie.

(STEVIE *seems quite calm now. He takes* WINNIE*'s arm and helps her on to the bus.*)

STEVIE: He's a good man, Mr Verloc.

INT. MAIN BEDROOM IN VERLOC'S HOUSE. NIGHT

VERLOC *stands, in his long underwear, his forehead pressed against the cool glass of the window, overlooking a cramped yard and the blank wall of an adjacent building. He looks preoccupied. His train of thought is interrupted by* WINNIE*'s* VOICE.

WINNIE: (*Off-screen*) Takings very small today.

(VERLOC *turns to look at her. She's in a snowy-white nightdress, brushing her hair.*)

VERLOC: That's the least of my worries.

(WINNIE *says nothing, waiting patiently for* VERLOC *to expand on this.*)

I've been called to a meeting tomorrow at the Russian Embassy. Can't be anything good.

WINNIE: Come to bed.

(VERLOC *lets down a venetian blind and plods wearily across the room; he stands opposite* WINNIE *and they turn down the bed.*)

VERLOC: I thought I was never going to get rid of them: all those wretches.

WINNIE: Mr Michaelis is a nice man.

VERLOC: He can afford to be: now he's found that old Duchess or whatever she is to support him. (*He looks across at* WINNIE, *eyes narrowed.*) And Ossipon?

(WINNIE *avoids answering, a slight constraint apparent in her expression.* VERLOC *registers this, smiling to himself as he clambers into bed.*)

He'll want for nothing as long as there are silly girls in the world with savings-bank books.

(WINNIE *snuggles up to him, her head on his chest, her expression preoccupied.*)

WINNIE: That boy isn't fit to hear what's said here. He doesn't know any better. He thinks it's all true.

(VERLOC *doesn't respond, locked in his own thoughts.*)

It's bad enough him having to get used to mother being gone. What did she want to go and do that for?

VERLOC: Perhaps it's just as well.

(*It's a neutral enough remark, but it seems to unsettle* WINNIE. *She rises up on one elbow and looks down at* VERLOC *anxiously*.)

WINNIE: He's such a good boy. I couldn't do without him.

(VERLOC *grunts, still half elsewhere.* WINNIE, *still anxious, reaches out to stroke his cheek*.)

Would you like . . . ?

(*She has his full attention now. They look at each other for a moment*.)

Or shall I put the light out?

(VERLOC *thinks for a moment: then he answers wearily*:)

VERLOC: Yes. Put it out.

(WINNIE *smiles, kisses him, reaches up and turns off the gas. Darkness*.)

EXT. BRETT STREET. DAY

VERLOC, *in his best blue overcoat with a velvet collar and brushed black bowler, steps out of his shop and, sighing in a demonstrative kind of way, raises his umbrella against the drizzle. He moves off down the grimy, crowded street, ignoring the beggars and street-criers and manœuvring his brilliantly shiny black boots through the mud with some care. He looks around him, his eyes bleary and disapproving.*

EXT. MOUNT STREET. DAY

Approaching Park Lane, the atmosphere is already far more salubrious. Hansoms jingle by, punctuated by the occasional private carriage, a two-horse brougham or a shiny victoria with a liveried coachman. VERLOC *tests the air cautiously, finds it's no longer raining and lowers his umbrella.*

EXT. HYDE PARK. DAY

VERLOC *waits, trying to find a gap in the ceaseless flow of riders and carriages passing through the park. Eventually he seizes his opportunity to slip across and vanishes down a slope, obscured by the traffic.*

EXT. BELGRAVIA. DAY

VERLOC *passes through the quiet stucco canyons of Belgravia. The winter sun washes the great white mansions gold; the street is deserted except for a butcher's boy with a barrow and a ruminative policeman. The contrast with the noise and squalor of Soho could scarcely be more marked: this is an entirely different world.*

VERLOC *comes to a halt outside the towering Embassy building. The Russian Imperial flag is fluttering outside it. He consults a piece of paper, checks up and down the street to make sure he's unobserved and then scuttles off towards the door of the Embassy.*

INT. EMBASSY. DAY

Seen from a great height, VERLOC *is shown into a vast reception area by a footman in a brown clawhammer coat. He pauses for a moment, overawed by the scale of the room, then hurries after the oblivious footman.*

INT. STAIRCASE. DAY

VERLOC, *his manner anxious, follows the footman up the broad marble staircase.*

INT. FIRST SECRETARY'S OFFICE. DAY

VERLOC *advances stolidly into the room as the footman pulls the doors to and disappears. The carpet is thick, the panelling opulent and the room, lit through three tall windows, appears to be empty.* VERLOC *looks around uncertainly, then turns to leave the room. He's interrupted by an unexpected* VOICE.

VOICE: Vous comprenez le français, je suppose.

(*The* VOICE *belongs to* VLADIMIR, *First Secretary at the Russian Embassy: his presence is revealed by two arms appearing either side of a large pink Biedermeier armchair.* VERLOC *replies, cautiously.*)

VERLOC: Oui. J'ai fait mon service militaire en France.

(VLADIMIR *rises, a youthful dandy with a trim red beard. He glances at a piece of paper and switches without comment to a light-accented English.*)

VLADIMIR: Ah, yes, you stole us the plans of the breech–block on their field-gun, did you not?

VERLOC: I did.

VLADIMIR: How much did you get for that?

VERLOC: Five years' hard labour.

VLADIMIR: That'll teach you to get caught.

(VERLOC *stares stoically back at him and after a pause* VLADIMIR *gestures at an entire wall of sofas and chairs.*)

Sit down.

(VERLOC *does so, making a particularly poor choice.*)

Now, you purport to be a desperate socialist or anarchist, am I right?

VERLOC: Anarchist.

VLADIMIR: Very corpulent for an anarchist, aren't you?

VERLOC: What's that?

VLADIMIR: An overweight anarchist seems to me to be something of a contradiction in terms.

(VERLOC *is rattled by this unexpected turn in the conversation. Now he watches as* VLADIMIR *springs lightly to his feet and begins moving around the room.*)

How long have you been drawing pay from this Embassy?

VERLOC: Eleven years.

VLADIMIR: I've read all the reports you sent to us last year; and I must say I'm at a loss to understand why you wrote them at all.

VERLOC: Only three months ago I gave you a warning of a plan

to assassinate the Grand Duke on his visit to Paris . . .

VLADIMIR: The French police assure us that your information was exaggerated and inaccurate: and don't shout.

(VERLOC *subsides sullenly.* VLADIMIR *moves to the large mirror on the mantelpiece and adjusts his old-fashioned cravat tied in a bow, whilst keeping a close eye on* VERLOC*'s reflection.*)

The secret service is, by its nature, difficult to describe. But I can certainly tell you what it is not: it is not a philanthropic institution. You are supposed to be an *agent provocateur*, but I can't think what you have provoked other than my irritation. I brought you in to tell you that from now on, I expect you to start earning your money. The good times are over. No work, no pay.

(*He turns to look directly at* VERLOC, *who is so taken aback, that all he can think of by way of reaction is to blow his nose, trumpeting violently into his handkerchief. Once this manoeuvre is complete, he looks up, flushed with anger.*)

VERLOC: You summoned me here with a most peremptory letter. This is only the third time I have been here in eleven years; and the first time I've arrived through the front door in broad daylight. You seem to have no regard for my safety whatsoever.

VLADIMIR: Your safety is your affair.

VERLOC: If I were seen coming here, it would destroy my usefulness.

VLADIMIR: If you cease to be useful, let me assure you of this, you shall be chucked.

(*Silence.* VLADIMIR *crosses to his desk and riffles through some papers.*)

I take it you know about the International Conference in Milan.

VERLOC: I read the newspapers.

VLADIMIR: Then you will have observed that the debate on the suppression of international terrorism has been entirely inconclusive. The British government in particular is reluctant to abandon its absurd and sentimental policy of offering asylum to so-called political refugees. Your damned friends have only to put in an application . . .

VERLOC: It means I can keep them all under my eye.

VLADIMIR: More to the point, I want them under lock and key. I want them handed back to us so we can deal with them properly. The absence of a . . . rational repression in this country is a scandal. I have decided that this is the correct psychological moment to provoke such a repression. This is why I have sent for you.

(VERLOC *is frowning at him, perplexed and apprehensive. But* VLADIMIR *takes his time, once again settling himself comfortably in the armchair.*)

What we need is a series of outrages: not necessarily sanguinary, I'm not a butcher, but startling. An attack, for example, on the fetish of the hour. Now, what do you suppose that might be?

VERLOC: Dunno.

(VLADIMIR *contemplates him with infinite distaste.*)

VLADIMIR: Then pay attention: I will try not to talk above your head. The class we are attacking is very difficult to shock. Conventional assassination they can take in their stride. A bomb in the National Gallery would create some effect, but principally among artists and art critics, people of no account. No, the sacrosanct fetish of the moment is science.

VERLOC: Science.

VLADIMIR: Unfortunately, it is not possible to throw a bomb into pure mathematics. And of course the practical details of the enterprise I leave to you. But I do have a suggestion.

VERLOC: I thought you might.

VLADIMIR: Yes, what do you say to having a go at astronomy?

VERLOC: Astronomy?

(VERLOC *frowns again, as if he's beginning to suspect that he is the victim of a particularly elaborate practical joke.* VLADIMIR *sits forward, meanwhile, a thin smile on his face.*)

EXT. GREENWICH OBSERVATORY. DAY

A SLOW PAN *across the green expanses of Greenwich Park ends with the discovery of the Observatory, perched on the crest of its hill, its gold weathercock catching the sun.*

VLADIMIR: (*Voice-over*) Everyone has heard of Greenwich. Even the bootblacks in Charing Cross Station. Nobody actually understands what it is, this new Greenwich Mean Time, but it has a mystical significance. The first meridian.

INT. FIRST SECRETARY'S OFFICE. DAY

VERLOC *looks up, sullen.*

VLADIMIR: An attack upon time itself. Entirely gratuitous and wonderfully inexplicable. If that doesn't stir the authorities in this country out of their cretinous torpor, I don't know what will.

VERLOC: It'll cost money.

VLADIMIR: Oh, no, that cock won't fight. You'll get your usual screw and if something doesn't happen very soon, you won't even get that. Do I make myself clear?

(VERLOC *doesn't answer immediately. Instead, he rises unhurriedly to his feet.*)

VERLOC: Is that all?

VLADIMIR: The Milan Conference reconvenes in a month. Unless you provide us before that time with a dynamite outrage, your connection with us is at an end. And now you may go.

(VERLOC *begins his long journey towards the door. Before he*

gets there, VLADIMIR *is on his feet and across the room to murmur in his ear with offensive intimacy.)*

The first meridian, Mr Verloc. Go for the first meridian.

EXT. GREENWICH PARK. DAY

VERLOC*'s bowler hat appears, followed immediately by his body, as he climbs a steep slope in Greenwich Park. The weather has turned overcast again and the area is deserted.* VERLOC *advances through the trees, squelching towards his goal: a side wall of the Observatory. He arrives at the wall and stops, peering furtively, first one way and then the other.*

INT. SITTING-ROOM IN VERLOC'S HOUSE. EVENING

The room of the political meeting also serves as the VERLOCS' *dining room.* VERLOC, *still wearing his overcoat and hat tipped back on his head, is morosely polishing off a plate of lamb stew and potatoes. He sits at the head of the table with* WINNIE *and* STEVIE *on either side of him. Both of them are anxiously aware of his profound displeasure.* VERLOC *takes his last mouthful and slams down his knife and fork.* WINNIE *collects his plate and takes it away.* STEVIE *stares at* VERLOC, *his mouth half-open: but* VERLOC *is oblivious to this. Eventually* WINNIE *returns and puts in front of him a steaming*

bowl of sponge pudding and custard. Wearily, he takes up his spoon.
WINNIE: Bad day?
VERLOC: Atrocious.
(VERLOC *decides to take off his hat. Before he can put it down,* STEVIE *has sprung to his feet and taken the hat, which he reverently carries downstairs. For the first time, something in* VERLOC*'s expression lightens.*)
WINNIE: He'd do anything for you, that boy, Adolf.

INT. MAIN BEDROOM. NIGHT

WINNIE, *in bed next to* VERLOC, *turns to him as he emits a profound sigh.*
WINNIE: What are you thinking about?
VERLOC: Emigrating . . .
WINNIE: What?
VERLOC: To France. Or California.
(*Silence.* WINNIE *is horrified.*)
WINNIE: I couldn't do that. You'd have to go by yourself.
(*He turns to look at her, as if roused from a dream.*)
And you couldn't do without me. Could you?
VERLOC: No. I couldn't.
(*His voice is hoarse with emotion. He reaches for her and enfolds her in a clumsy embrace. She smiles at him as he begins to fumble with her nightdress.*)

INT. TOP LANDING. DAY

VERLOC *emerges from the bedroom and stops in his tracks. What's startled him is the sight of* STEVIE, *sitting on the floor in front of the grandfather clock, his eyes wide and staring, his chin on his knees.* VERLOC *seems about to speak to him, but thinks better of it, passes in front of him and sets off down the stairs.*

INT. SHOP. DAY

WINNIE *sits behind the counter in the deserted shop. She looks up as she hears* VERLOC*'s footstep on the staircase.*
VERLOC: He's up there moping on the landing again.
WINNIE: It's all along of mother leaving.
VERLOC: I'm going out.
WINNIE: Why don't you take him with you?

(VERLOC *hesitates, caught unawares by this suggestion.*)
Fresh air would do him good.

EXT. STREET IN ISLINGTON. DAY

STEVIE *stands under a lamppost waiting, like a dog outside a supermarket, looking up and down the muddy street, disfigured with bits of straw and waste paper, eddying in the gusty wind. He hugs himself against the cold and looks up at a shabby terraced house.*

INT. STAIRCASE. DAY

VERLOC *follows the* PROFESSOR *up the stairs. At a certain point, the frayed stair-carpet expires and the men's footsteps echo on the bare wood. The* PROFESSOR *is wearing a tattered maroon dressing-gown.*

INT. VERLOC'S SHOP. EVENING

VERLOC *is behind the counter, breaking open cardboard cartons. These contain various obscene publications from France, which he hands over the counter to* WINNIE, *without so much as glancing at them. She, equally incurious, distributes them along an empty shelf.* VERLOC*'s mood has considerably improved.*

VERLOC: I had a letter from Michaelis today.

WINNIE: Oh, yes?

VERLOC: His Duchess has given him the use of a country cottage. To finish his book, if you please. And he's offered to put up Stevie for a few days.

WINNIE: That's nice of him.

VERLOC: But I don't suppose you could do without him.

WINNIE: Well, of course I could. If it was somewhere he wanted to go. Why not?
(VERLOC *frowns briefly at an enormous-breasted Valkyrie with a riding-crop, then passes the pile of magazines to* WINNIE.)

VERLOC: I'll take him down, then.

EXT. BRETT STREET. DAY

WINNIE *stands in the doorway of the shop, her arms around* STEVIE. VERLOC *stands nearby, holding a small suitcase. Eventually,* WINNIE *disengages from the embrace.*

WINNIE: Goodbye, darling.
(STEVIE *stretches out his arms and takes* WINNIE*'s face*

between his hands. He contemplates her, his expression serious.)

STEVIE: I love you, Winn.

WINNIE: Off you go.

(*Obediently,* STEVIE *releases her and sets off down the sordid street with* VERLOC. *They're identically dressed in dark overcoats and bowlers, which makes them look a little like Laurel and Hardy.*

CLOSE *on* WINNIE, *as she watches them go, murmuring to herself.*)

Like father and son.

(*And indeed, that's what they look like, from* WINNIE*'s* POV, *through the glass door of the shop, as they move down the street, away from her.*)

INT. SILENUS RESTAURANT. DAY

A large basement room, its tables covered with red-and-white check tablecloths, its walls decorated with a crude fresco of kitsch medieval revelry. At the foot of the stairs is a mechanical piano. The camera contemplates this for a moment and it suddenly bursts into a maniacal waltz tune, the keys successively depressing in ghostly automatic clusters.

At a corner table, pressed against the wall is the PROFESSOR, *nursing a pint of cloudy beer.* OSSIPON *faces him, sipping a glass of red wine.*

OSSIPON: Do you give your stuff to anybody who wants it?

PROFESSOR: I never refuse anybody. I make it an absolute rule.

(*Slightly unexpectedly, he has an American accent. He gulps at his beer and looks at* OSSIPON, *his expression icily calm, behind his round spectacles.*)

As long as I have a pinch left over for myself.

OSSIPON: And you think this is a sound principle?

PROFESSOR: Perfectly.

OSSIPON: You mean you'd sell to the police?

PROFESSOR: They leave me alone.

OSSIPON: Couldn't they arrest you if they wanted to?

PROFESSOR: What for?

OSSIPON: Dealing in explosives without a licence.

(*The* PROFESSOR *permits himself a thin and contemptuous smile.*)

PROFESSOR: It is very well known to the police that I never part with the final handful of my wares.

(*He taps his breast pocket very lightly.*)

I carry it right here. Next to my heart.

(*He unbuttons his waistcoat to reveal glass tubes on a leather patch, strapped against his chest.*)

OSSIPON: What if six policemen jump on you in the street?

(*The* PROFESSOR *moves his hand to the left-hand pocket of his jacket.*)

PROFESSOR: In this pocket I have an indiarubber bulb. I always walk with my hand closed around it.

(*He takes the black bulb out of his pocket and shows it to* OSSIPON.)

If I squeeze it, it activates a detonator, which works on the same principle as the shutter of a camera lens.

OSSIPON: Instantaneous?

PROFESSOR: Unfortunately not. I estimate ten seconds would elapse between applying the pressure and the explosion.

OSSIPON: Ten seconds! It's a lifetime.

PROFESSOR: I'm working on it. I'm trying to invent a detonator that would adjust itself to all conditions without loss of reliability. A perfectly precise mechanism. A really intelligent detonator. (*He looks across the room, his expression complacent.*) But this isn't so bad. You see that couple going up the stairs?

(OSSIPON *glances over his shoulder and nods in acknowledgement.*)

This would finish them. And everyone else in the room.

(*The mechanical piano stops abruptly, in mid-phrase. The* PROFESSOR *leans forward minimally.*)

Character, you see. That's all that counts. Force of personality.

OSSIPON: Suppose you meet a policeman of character?

PROFESSOR: It would be a character based on conventional morality and dependent on life, in other words inhibited and infinitely vulnerable: I depend on something, which knows no restraint and cannot be attacked. Death.

OSSIPON: I've never understood what it is you want.

PROFESSOR: Only one thing: a perfect detonator.

(*He sits back again, finishes his beer and beckons a waiter. The mechanical piano begins again, a mazurka this time. The* PROFESSOR *indicates more drinks should be brought; then, he looks across the table at* OSSIPON.)

It's a precise aim. Not like your committees and delegations and revolutions, which are simply a mirror image of the society you pretend to despise.

(*The waiter arrives with the drinks. The piano rattles on.* OSSIPON *waits for a moment, then leans forward himself, his voice husky with suppressed excitement.*)

OSSIPON: Did you know there was a man blown up in Greenwich Park this morning?

PROFESSOR: No.

OSSIPON: Huge explosion around half-past eleven. Fragments of body all over the place. Here you are, the usual newspaper gup.

(*He takes a rolled newspaper out of his pocket and hands it across the table. He watches the* PROFESSOR *closely for a reaction, but the latter merely runs his eyes over the story and then lays down the paper, expressionless.*)

Criminal stupidity.

PROFESSOR: I don't know what you mean by criminal.

OSSIPON: What everybody else means. I mean a thing like this is very dangerous for people in our position. And you tell me you're giving your stuff away to any fool who asks for it.

PROFESSOR: With both hands. Freely. Because what's needed is a clean sweep. And I couldn't give a damn about the consequences.

OSSIPON: Can you describe the person you gave the explosives to?

PROFESSOR: Describe him? Yes. I can describe him in one word. Verloc.

(*Once again, the piano breaks off in mid-phrase.* OSSIPON *slumps back in his seat, astonished.*)

OSSIPON: Verloc?

INT. STAIRCASE. DAY

The PROFESSOR *leads* VERLOC *up the uncarpeted stairs and unlocks a door at the top of the house.*

PROFESSOR: (*Voice-over*) He said he wanted it for some kind of demonstration against a building.

INT. THE PROFESSOR'S ROOM. DAY

VERLOC *follows the* PROFESSOR *into his small, shabby bed-sitting-room, unremarkable except that it contains a wardrobe so large, it's hard to imagine how it could have been fitted through the door. The portable bomb lies, recognizable, on the* PROFESSOR*'s desk. There's a heavy padlock on the wardrobe; and* VERLOC *waits, as the* PROFESSOR *takes a key from his dressing-gown pocket and unlocks the padlock.*

PROFESSOR: (*Voice-over*) And he wanted to be able to carry it in public without arousing suspicion. So I cut the bottom out of an old one-gallon copal varnish can. Afterwards I re-soldered it. I put the detonator in the screw cap.

OSSIPON: (*Voice-over*) What do you suppose happened?

INT. SILENUS RESTAURANT. DAY

The PROFESSOR *shrugs, indifferent.*

PROFESSOR: I don't know. Once you tighten the cap and make the connection, it gives you twenty minutes; and it also becomes extremely volatile. So I guess he either ran the time too close or let it fall.

(*The* PROFESSOR *rises to his feet and starts climbing into his tattered overcoat.*)

OSSIPON: I can't imagine what came over Verloc. He was a nonentity, a quite ordinary personality. Useful, but no more. Married, even. Ran a shop, which I imagine his wife started for him. He didn't tell you why?

PROFESSOR: I didn't ask.

(*He bangs a few coins down on the table. The piano starts up again, with a selection of patriotic airs.* OSSIPON *shakes his head, troubled.*)

OSSIPON: I don't know what I should do.

PROFESSOR: What you usually do, I imagine.

(OSSIPON *looks up at him, interrogatively.*)

Fasten yourself on the woman for all she's worth.

(*He turns abruptly and walks away from the table, so that* OSSIPON*'s protest dies on his lips.*)

EXT. STREET. DAY

It's the middle of the afternoon and what little light there is on this overcast day is beginning to die. The PROFESSOR *moves through a busy throng of pedestrians, the camera* CLOSE *on his face, registering his icy distaste. At a certain moment, he ducks out of the crowd into a narrow side-alley.*

EXT. ALLEY. DAY

The alley is a short connection between two busy streets, but at the moment it's more or less deserted. On one side is a row of abandoned houses (black holes for windows, the gardens overgrown scrub), while on the other is a number of dingy shops. The largest of these is a second-hand furniture shop, whose contents have spilled out into and across the alley, sofas, chairs, wash-stands, a cheval mirror, unevenly distributed in the open air.

As the PROFESSOR *approaches the narrow reaches of this unchaperoned agglomeration of furniture, he stiffens. Moving towards him is a stalwart, fair man with long moustaches the colour of ripe corn. He wears a hat and dark overcoat and carries a furled umbrella and slows down as soon as he sees the* PROFESSOR. *He is*

CHIEF INSPECTOR HEAT *of the Special Crimes Department.*

HEAT: Well, well, well.

(*The* PROFESSOR *comes to a halt, close to a long, battered sofa. His left hand moves instinctively to his jacket pocket in a movement which does not go unobserved by* HEAT.)

PROFESSOR: Chief Inspector Heat.

HEAT: It's all right. I'm not looking for you. Not this time.

(*The* PROFESSOR *doesn't answer: instead, he uncovers his gums in a mirthless, silent laugh.*)

When I am, I shall know where to find you.

PROFESSOR: And I'm sure your obituary will be more flattering than you deserve. Also, however conscientiously your friends may try to sort us out, I'm afraid some of you may end up being buried with some of me.

HEAT: This sort of stuff is all very well for frightening children.

(*Much to* HEAT*'s surprise, the* PROFESSOR *suddenly leaps across on to the sofa, still keeping his hand in his pocket.*)

PROFESSOR: There's no time like the present. You'll never have a more favourable opportunity for a humane arrest. Just you and me. There isn't even a cat around. Surely it would be a worthwhile self-sacrifice for a public servant.

(*His tone of light banter changes suddenly and he becomes deadly serious. He brings the black bulb out of his pocket.*)

You'd do it, if you knew how cruelly tempted I am, every time I walk through a crowd.

HEAT: If I was to grab you now, I'd be no better than you.

PROFESSOR: You'll never get me so cheap.

HEAT: I don't know what your game is: I don't expect you know yourself.

PROFESSOR: You're rather famous for not understanding what our game is.

HEAT: Well, whatever it is, give it up.

(*The* PROFESSOR *shakes his head, a thin smile on his lips. The bulb has disappeared, back into his pocket.*)

You'll find we are too many for you.

(HEAT *turns away from the prone figure of the* PROFESSOR, *switching easily on to another tack.*)

Just as well you people always make such a mess of things.

If a burglar was that incompetent, he'd starve.

(*The* PROFESSOR *rises to his feet: he speaks with a venomous quiet.*)

PROFESSOR: I'm better at my work than you are.

HEAT: That's quite enough of that.

(*The* PROFESSOR *laughs again, out loud this time, and moves off abruptly.* HEAT *watches him for a moment, then turns and begins striding away from him, muttering to himself.*)

Lunatic.

EXT. SCOTLAND YARD. EVENING

It's raining by now and darkness has fallen. HEAT *hurries across the forecourt of Scotland Yard, his umbrella up. He's greeted deferentially by the doorman, as befits a popular and successful officer.*

INT. THE ASSISTANT COMMISSIONER'S OFFICE. EVENING

The ASSISTANT COMMISSIONER OF POLICE *is a tall, slim man, too dark to be very English-looking and apparently younger than* HEAT. *He sits behind a vast, paper-strewn desk. Its large wooden armchair is festooned with speaking-tubes. He goes on writing as* HEAT *enters the room and speaks without looking up.*

ASST COMMISSIONER: Please make yourself comfortable, Chief Inspector.

HEAT: Thank you, sir.

(*He's left his overcoat and umbrella somewhere outside; now he waits patiently until the* ASSISTANT COMMISSIONER *finishes writing and looks up, slightly irritated to find* HEAT *still on his feet.*)

ASST COMMISSIONER: Sit down.

(*He stares at* HEAT *as the latter finds a seat and settles himself; and continues staring at him for a moment.* HEAT *endures the scrutiny quite calmly.*)

A couple of weeks ago you assured me there was no prospect whatsoever of any outbreak of anarchist activity. I passed this on to the Home Secretary. He was extremely pleased. He smiled at me. I wonder if you can imagine how annoying I find the memory of that smile?

HEAT: None of our lot had anything to do with this.

(*The* ASSISTANT COMMISSIONER *considers this remark for a moment, then proceeds in a matter-of-fact tone.*)

ASST COMMISSIONER: Tell me what you discovered in Greenwich.

EXT. MAZE HILL STATION. DAY

Seen from inside a compartment of a stationary train, a stream of passengers move down the platform towards the barrier. One of them is VERLOC. *As he passes the window, the train begins to move in the same direction and stays level with him for a moment, before overtaking him and moving out of frame.* VERLOC *is revealed to be holding a yellow tin can. He looks back over his shoulder, frowning with impatience.*

HEAT: (*Voice-over*) Our man arrived at Maze Hill station at 11.08 on the Gravesend train. Short, stocky fellow. He was carrying a tin can.

EXT. STATION BARRIER. DAY

The camera, at waist-level, sees an official collect two tickets from an unidentifiable hand. Part of the tin can also appears in the frame.

HEAT: (*Voice-over*) As a matter of fact, there was two of them. They'd come up from a place called Aldington. Near Hythe. An old woman saw them making their way towards the Observatory.

EXT. KING WILLIAM STREET LODGE. DAY

A constable is talking to the park-keeper. Suddenly, behind them, there's the dull thud and the dark smoke-plume of an explosion. The constable sets off at a run in the direction of the explosion.

HEAT: (*Voice-over*) The explosion happened about ten minutes later. A constable heard it: he was on the scene within a minute or two.

EXT. GREENWICH PARK. DAY

HEAT *stands among a few officials, policemen and passers-by, above a deep crater of raw earth. He turns and sets off in the direction of a large oak-tree.*

ASST COMMISSIONER: (*Voice-over*) What evidence do we have that it was the same people?

HEAT: (*Voice-over*) Strips of yellow tin in the vicinity.

(*And* HEAT *is now prying a sharp piece of tin out of the oak-tree's bark. It's difficult, because the tin is so deeply embedded; and* HEAT *leans his left hand against the tree for support. He becomes aware of something; and he looks at his left hand, now smeared with blood. We take his* POV *and pan up the tree; the whole trunk is spattered with thick, bloody gobbets.*)

Only one of them was killed.

INT. ASSISTANT COMMISSIONER'S OFFICE. EVENING

The ASSISTANT COMMISSIONER *looks sharply across at* HEAT.

ASST COMMISSIONER: How do you know?

HEAT: Bits and pieces only added up to one body. Couldn't identify him, but he had the right number of everything.

INT. MORTUARY. DAY

HEAT, *flanked by the constable and a laboratory assistant, holds up the waterproof sheet to reveal a foot, still wearing its sock and polished boot, but severed at mid-shin and protruding from a hideous mess, which resembles the ingredients of a cannibal's feast.*

HEAT: (*Voice-over*) Good deal of him they had to scrape up with a spade.

(HEAT *puffs out his cheeks and exhales noisily, dropping the sheet back to cover the remains.*)

INT. ASSISTANT COMMISSIONER'S OFFICE. EVENING

HEAT *shakes his head and adds half-humorously*:

HEAT: Nice treat for the coroner's jury.

(*By now, the* ASSISTANT COMMISSIONER *is standing at the window. Outside, it's pouring with rain, the gas-lamps blurred by the amounts of water cascading down the window-pane.*

ASST COMMISSIONER: Filthy weather.

(HEAT *chooses not to respond: the* ASSISTANT COMMISSIONER *turns back to look at him.*)

The Home Secretary said he'd been told we were very efficient and what we seemed most efficient at was making him look a fool.

(HEAT *takes this aboard: he decides the moment has come to help the discussion forward.*)

HEAT: There is one what you might call chink of light, sir.

(*The* ASSISTANT COMMISSIONER *resumes his seat. He waits.*)

This place in Kent. Aldington. Near Hythe.

ASST COMMISSIONER: Yes? Odd sort of place of origin for two ruthless terrorists, wouldn't you say?

HEAT: Not if you happen to know that not more than a mile away is a cottage, occupied at present by the ex-convict Michaelis.

(*Silence. The* ASSISTANT COMMISSIONER *seems far from pleased.*)

ASST COMMISSIONER: I thought you just told me our anarchists had nothing to do with this affair.

HEAT: Doesn't mean we can't issue a charge if we feel like it.

ASST COMMISSIONER: You'll need some pretty conclusive evidence.

HEAT: Oh, I don't think that'd be too difficult, sir. I can look after that. Trust me for that.

(*He permits himself a complacent smile: which disappears quickly when he becomes aware that the* ASSISTANT COMMISSIONER, *far from responding to his reassurance, is starting to look even more displeased. Slightly unnerved, he begins to bluster.*)

Man like that has no business being out of prison, if you ask me. Nor do any of them. I tell you, sir, makes me long for the days when I was catching good, honest thieves. You know where you are with thieves. Bit of mutual respect. And at least they're . . . normal.

(*The* ASSISTANT COMMISSIONER *has been frowning during this speech, concentrating very hard, but not on what* HEAT *is saying. Now he decides to trust his instinct.*)

ASST COMMISSIONER: I believe you're hiding something from me, Chief Inspector.

(HEAT*'s look of injured indignation doesn't entirely conceal a flash of guilt.*)

INT. MORTUARY. DAY

Unnoticed by the laboratory assistant, HEAT *leans forward, twitches back the sheet, picks something out of the bloody mess and pockets it.*

ASST COMMISSIONER: (*Voice-over*) What is it?

HEAT: (*Voice-over*) Something with regards to Michaelis, sir?

ASST COMMISSIONER: (*Voice-over*) No; what's puzzling me in fact is your eagerness to shunt the whole train off into a siding marked Michaelis.

INT. ASSISTANT COMMISSIONER'S OFFICE. EVENING

HEAT *plucks briefly at the stiff collar of his shirt, as if the room has suddenly become too warm for him.*

ASST COMMISSIONER: So you'd better tell me what else you have discovered.

(HEAT *is wrestling with his reluctance to say anything more. Finally, he decides he has to take the plunge.*)

HEAT: As a matter of fact, there was another matter I had intended to draw to your attention in due course. I found an address.

ASST COMMISSIONER: An address?

HEAT: That's right, sir. On the corpse.

ASST COMMISSIONER: What address?

HEAT: 32, Brett Street. It's a shop.

ASST COMMISSIONER: What kind of shop?

HEAT: The kind of shop you might expect to find in Soho, sir.

ASST COMMISSIONER: Who runs this shop?

HEAT: A man who, from time to time, I have occasion to make use of.

ASST COMMISSIONER: Does he have a name, this paragon?

HEAT: Verloc.

(Silence. The ASSISTANT COMMISSIONER *waits.* HEAT *clears his throat.)*

Personal friend of mine in the French Police tipped me the wink that he was a secret agent in the pay of the Russian Embassy. So I called on him one evening and told him who I was. He didn't bat an eyelid. Said he was a married man and didn't want any trouble. So we came to an arrangement.

ASST COMMISSIONER: Describe it.

HEAT: I had a word with the Customs people, made sure they wouldn't interfere with any of his shipments; and in return I'm able to consult him whenever I think there's something in the wind.

ASST COMMISSIONER: And how long has this been going on?

HEAT: Seven years.

ASST COMMISSIONER: No wonder your reputation for omniscience is so established.

(It's clear from HEAT*'s expression that he considers this remark beneath contempt. He leaves it unanswered. The* ASSISTANT COMMISSIONER *gets up again and begins moving around the room.)*

So in other words, you would rather throw an innocent man to the lions than dispense with the services of so useful an informant.

HEAT: I would hardly describe Michaelis as innocent, sir: even though I know he enjoys a number of influential friends, sir.

ASST COMMISSIONER: If you mean the Duchess of . . .

HEAT: Isn't she a particular friend of your wife's, sir?

(With this, he has hit home: but the ASSISTANT COMMISSIONER *makes a swift recovery.)*

ASST COMMISSIONER: As to that, the First Secretary at the Russian Embassy is a member of my club. And I may say, it's most improper of you to try finessing with me in this way. This Verloc is a spy in the pay of a foreign embassy: I don't feel disposed to overlook that fact just because he may privately be of service to you.

HEAT: It's my opinion he knows nothing at all of this business.

ASST COMMISSIONER: Then how do you account for the address?

HEAT: I don't account for it.

(*His jaw sets in a stubborn line.*)

ASST COMMISSIONER: You see, I begin to see this as a heaven-sent opportunity to deal with a whole gang of spies, *agents provocateurs* and all kinds of political riff-raff.

(HEAT *adopts an air of elaborate indifference; which causes the* ASSISTANT COMMISSIONER *to take a different, entirely businesslike tone.*)

You may go: report to me here at nine o'clock tomorrow morning.

HEAT: As you please, sir.

(*He rises and leaves the room abruptly. The* ASSISTANT COMMISSIONER *looks out of the window and briskly gathers up his hat, gloves and umbrella.*)

EXT. EXPLORERS' CLUB. NIGHT

It's still raining heavily; and the ASSISTANT COMMISSIONER *stands on the terrace of his club, looking out into the street. He sees something and straightens up.*

His POV*: below, descending from his official carriage, is* VLADIMIR*, smoking a large cigar.*

The ASSISTANT COMMISSIONER *moves through the archway and intercepts* VLADIMIR *on the covered stone stairway; the latter extends a hand, apparently delighted to see him.*

VLADIMIR: Harold! Just the man I was hoping to run across.

ASST COMMISSIONER: How are you?

(*His tone is dry, but not unfriendly.*)

VLADIMIR: Will you take a drink with me?

ASST COMMISSIONER: Unfortunately, I have an errand to run.

VLADIMIR: Busy day, uh? With this outrage in Greenwich Park?

ASST COMMISSIONER: Just so.

VLADIMIR: I have said this before: I cannot understand why your government is so indulgent towards these terrorists. Perhaps it is because your country does not suffer as cruelly from their activities as we do in my country.

(*He sucks on his cigar. The* ASSISTANT COMMISSIONER *considers him for a moment and then speaks with a lethal quiet.*)

ASST COMMISSIONER: We are on the track of a man called Verloc.

VLADIMIR: What?

ASST COMMISSIONER: I understand you know him.

VLADIMIR: What makes you think that?

ASST COMMISSIONER: He has no secrets from us.

VLADIMIR: A lying dog of some kind.

(*He throws away his cigar and turns away towards the sanctuary of the club. The* ASSISTANT COMMISSIONER *restrains him with a hand on his sleeve.*)

ASST COMMISSIONER: This may well be the breakthrough we've been waiting for.

VLADIMIR: What do you mean?

ASST COMMISSIONER: In our campaign to clear out of this country the despicable scum that use embassies as a cover for their criminal activities.

VLADIMIR: I have an appointment.

ASST COMMISSIONER: I believe I've heard you complain of the inefficiency of our police: but within eight hours of this explosion, we seem to have established not only the perpetrator, but even the instigator behind him. Not bad, wouldn't you say?

(VLADIMIR, *evidently flustered, turns to go back down the stairs, but the* ASSISTANT COMMISSIONER *is blocking his way.*)

Aren't you impressed?

(VLADIMIR *pushes past him, shooting him a furious glance, and scrambles back into the waiting carriage. A flash of lightning illuminates* VLADIMIR, *as he issues frenzied instructions to the driver. And, as the thunder explodes, the* ASSISTANT COMMISSIONER *stands watching the carriage pull away, extremely gratified at the effect of his needling.*)

INT./EXT. SHOP. NIGHT

As the thunder echoes, WINNIE *looks up from her bookkeeping. She's sitting behind the counter, making entries in a heavy black ledger. She's scratching away with her pen, when suddenly there's an exceptionally vivid flash of lightning.* WINNIE *looks up with a*

sharp intake of breath; her hand flies to her mouth.

WINNIE*'s* POV*: framed in the window, staring in at her, wild-eyed, dripping with rain, his face frozen in a ghastly expression, is* VERLOC.

As the thunder crashes, he opens the door and the bell clatters. WINNIE *is on her way round the counter to greet him.*

VERLOC *stares at her blankly. Drips cascade from the rim of his bowler hat.*

WINNIE: Where's your umbrella?

VERLOC: Must have left it somewhere.

WINNIE: Have you been down to see Stevie?

(VERLOC *looks at her for a moment, in some kind of paralysis.*)

VERLOC: No.

(*He breaks away and sets off up the stairs, still wearing his hat and coat.* WINNIE *frowns, puzzled by his abrupt departure. She reflects for a moment, closes up the ledger and puts it away, and starts up the steps herself.*)

INT. SITTING-ROOM. NIGHT

WINNIE *arrives at the top of the stairs to find the room in darkness, except for the subdued glow of the fire. She hesitates a moment, then fetches out a matchbox and approaches one of the gas-lamps. She's about to strike a match, when she freezes, suddenly aware of an extraordinary, unidentifiable sound: a kind of low clicking, very rapid and sinister. She strikes a match and lights the lamp.*

WINNIE*'s* POV*: at first, she can't see where the sound is coming from; all she's aware of immediately are* VERLOC*'s overcoat, thrown untidily across the sofa; and his hat, nearby on the floor. But the sound continues and the camera pans, as she moves her head, to reveal an alarming sight:* VERLOC*, hunched up on a chair pulled up to the fire, his feet right inside the fender, his head between his hands and almost down on his lap. The sound is the violent and convulsive chatter of his teeth, which is causing his whole body to shudder uncontrollably.*

WINNIE *lights a second lamp and then moves across to* VERLOC*, concerned.*

WINNIE: You've let yourself get soaked through.
VERLOC: I'm all right.
WINNIE: You'll be laid up with a cold, next thing.
VERLOC: No, I'll be all right.

(*He makes an enormous, not altogether successful effort to control the chattering of his teeth.*)

WINNIE: I'll get the tea on.

(*She moves away into the kitchen, which is off to one side.* VERLOC *sits up and gradually manages to overcome his shuddering. His teeth are gritted now, his face a mask of effort and profound misery.* WINNIE *returns with a tray on which are a tablecloth, two plates, two knives and forks, two cups and saucers, bread, butter and a jar of pickled onions. She sets out the tablecloth and starts laying the table.*)

Where've you been all day anyway?

VERLOC: Nowhere.

(WINNIE *seems not to find his answer unsatisfactory. She returns to the kitchen and re-emerges with a pinkish joint of cold beef on a plate with a carving knife and fork and a matching steel.*)

I did go to the bank.

WINNIE: What for?
VERLOC: Draw out the money.
WINNIE: What, all of it?
VERLOC: All of it, yes.

WINNIE: Why?

VERLOC: Thought I might need it.

WINNIE: I don't understand.

(VERLOC *leans forward again, holding his hands out towards the fire.*)

VERLOC: You can trust me, you know that, don't you?

WINNIE: Oh, yes, I trust you.

(*She sharpens the carving knife on the steel in a vigorous movement.*)

If I hadn't trusted you, I wouldn't have married you.

(*She puts down the carving knife and steel, looking across at him. Still bowed forward over the fire, he turns his face to her. He looks at her with an expression of such naked distress, that she moves across the room, concerned, arrives behind his chair, puts her arms around his broad back and lays her cheek against the top of his head.*)

And you're all right with me, aren't you?

(*She turns her face to kiss him on the temple.*)

Not tired of me yet?

(*Suddenly,* VERLOC *surges tempestuously to his feet and grasps* WINNIE *to him in a fervent embrace. After a while, this turns into a kiss.* WINNIE *overcomes her surprise and begins to respond to something desperate in his greedy kisses. Finally, he lifts her off her feet, carries her over to the sofa and stretches her out on it. His eyes are glazed with passion, as he begins tearing at her clothes. This is interrupted by the sound of the shop bell downstairs.*)

Shop, Adolf.

VERLOC: What?

(*He sits up, as if coming to.* WINNIE *starts to reassemble her clothing.*)

WINNIE: You'd better go.

(*For a moment,* VERLOC *continues to look bewildered: then he rises, shakes himself like a dog, lumbers over to the stairs and vanishes.* WINNIE *takes some time to make herself decent, then, suddenly curious, sets off towards the staircase herself.*)

INT. STAIRCASE. NIGHT

The camera accompanies WINNIE *down the stairs.*

INT. SHOP. NIGHT

WINNIE'*s* POV*:* VERLOC *and whoever was at the door come gradually into view, feet first. Finally, as* WINNIE *reaches the foot of the stairs, both men turn to look at her.* VERLOC'*s face is papery white, blank with shock; and the visitor turns out to be the* ASSISTANT COMMISSIONER.

ANOTHER ANGLE *shows* WINNIE *approaching, concerned at* VERLOC'*s appearance.*

WINNIE: Are you feeling all right?

VERLOC: I find I'll have to go out this evening.

(*Abruptly, he brushes past her and vanishes up the stairs.* WINNIE *frowns briefly at the* ASSISTANT COMMISSIONER, *who acknowledges her with a little bow.*)

WINNIE: You over from the Continent?

(*The* ASSISTANT COMMISSIONER'*s response is a brief, enigmatic smile.*)

You do understand English?

ASST COMMISSIONER: Oh, yes, I understand English.

WINNIE: Did you know Mr Verloc in France, perhaps?

ASST COMMISSIONER: I've heard of him.

(*A thought occurs to* WINNIE *and, excusing herself with a brusque nod, she turns and starts up the stairs again.*)

INT. STAIRCASE. NIGHT

WINNIE *hurries upstairs.*

INT. SITTING-ROOM. NIGHT

VERLOC *stands, in his overcoat, propping himself up on a table with both arms, as if winded.*

WINNIE: Adolf.

(*He looks at her, as if emerging from a trance.*)

You're not going out with all that money on you?

VERLOC: Money?

(*He looks completely blank for a moment, then suddenly remembers.*)

Oh. Yes. No.

(*He takes a brand-new pigskin wallet out of his pocket and hands it to her.*)

WINNIE: Do you know that man?

VERLOC: I've heard of him.

(*He goes to pick up his hat from down by the sofa, grunting with the effort.*)

WINNIE: He's not one of those Embassy people you were talking about?

(VERLOC *straightens up, angrily ramming his hat on his head.*)

VERLOC: Embassy people! I could cut their hearts out, soon as look at them!

WINNIE: You get rid of him as quick as you can and come back home to me. You want looking after.

(VERLOC*, soothed by her words, sets off down the stairs again. When he's gone,* WINNIE *peeks into the wallet. She's amazed by the thickness of the wad of banknotes. She looks around, searching for a place to stow the wallet, dismissing various obvious alternatives. From below, the sound of the shop bell. Another moment's indecision and then she slips the wallet into her pocket.*)

EXT. BRETT STREET. NIGHT

The storm has somewhat abated, but there's still a blustery wind and a driving cold rain. VERLOC *and the* ASSISTANT COMMISSIONER *move down the mud-streaked pavement, skirting the worst puddles.*

ASST COMMISSIONER: I can only help you if you tell me everything, you understand that, don't you?

VERLOC: I'll tell you everything.

(*They move on down the street and turn the corner, the* ASSISTANT COMMISSIONER *following* VERLOC*'s lead.*)

INT. SHOP. NIGHT

WINNIE *has resumed work on the accounts. She looks up as the bell goes and* HEAT *lets himself into the shop.* WINNIE *frowns, half-recognizing him and trying fruitlessly to place him; he smiles pleasantly at her.*

HEAT: Husband in by any chance, Mrs Verloc?

WINNIE: No, he's gone out.

HEAT: I wanted a word with him.

(*No response from* WINNIE. HEAT *stands there for a moment before resuming.*)

I'd wait if I thought he wasn't going to be too long.

(*Once again,* WINNIE *volunteers nothing. An edge of irritation is beginning to creep into* HEAT*'s voice.*)

Any idea where he's gone?

WINNIE: He didn't say.

(*She looks down at the ledger again.* HEAT *contemplates her, momentarily perplexed.*)

HEAT: I think you know who I am.

(WINNIE *looks up again, perfectly calm.*)

I'm a policeman, you know that.

WINNIE: I try not to bother my head about these things.

HEAT: My name is Heat. Chief Inspector Heat of the Special Crimes Department.

WINNIE: Oh, yes.

(*Silence.* HEAT *searches for a way forward.*)

HEAT: So your husband didn't say when he'd be back?

WINNIE: He's out with someone.

HEAT: A friend?

WINNIE: No. Just someone who called.

HEAT: Would you mind telling me what this someone looked like?

WINNIE: Tall, thin fellow. Sort of foreign-looking.

HEAT: Well, damn it, I thought as much.

(*He suppresses his surge of anger as best he can.*)

In that case, I think I won't wait for your husband.

(WINNIE *seems unmoved by this news. She looks placidly across at* HEAT.)

You're very calm, but I expect you could give me a pretty good idea of what's going on, if you felt like it.

WINNIE: What is going on?

(HEAT *gives up: he turns and begins to leave the shop. Then, as an afterthought, he turns back in the doorway.*)

HEAT: There is something else, a small matter, perhaps you might be able to help us?

WINNIE: Yes?

HEAT: We've come into possession of a . . . what we believe might be a stolen overcoat.

WINNIE: We're not missing an overcoat.

(HEAT *moves back into the shop, far enough to pick up a bottle of purple marking ink from one of the shelves. He holds the bottle up to the light.*)

HEAT: In the overcoat is a label, with this address written in purple marking ink.

(*For the first time,* WINNIE *seems concerned. She leans forward across the counter.*)

WINNIE: Well, then, that must be my brother's.

HEAT: Could I have a word with him?

WINNIE: He's not here.

HEAT: Where is he?

WINNIE: Staying with a friend in the country.

HEAT: Has he got a name, this friend?

WINNIE: Michaelis.

(HEAT *lets out a low, triumphant whistle. He moves back towards* WINNIE.)

HEAT: Excellent. Yes. Now we're talking.

INT. BEDROOM IN THE CONTINENTAL HOTEL. NIGHT

A sordid room in a short-term Soho hotel. There's one greasy armchair, in which VERLOC *is slumped, a wardrobe with a mirror and a grubby, iron-frame single bed. The* ASSISTANT COMMISSIONER*'s coat is thrown across the bed; he paces up and down, interrogating* VERLOC.

ASST COMMISSIONER: So Michaelis had nothing whatever to do with this affair?

VERLOC: No. It's just that Stevie, my . . . brother-in-law, was staying in his house in the country. I collected him about eight this morning and told Michaelis I'd bring him back tonight.

EXT. MAZE HILL STATION. DAY

VERLOC, *the tin can in his hand, turns back to look down the platform.* STEVIE *is loitering about twenty yards behind, looking up at something which has caught his interest.* VERLOC *gestures to him; then he's obliged to walk back and take him by the arm to march him down towards the barrier.*

VERLOC: (*Voice-over*) We took the train up to Maze Hill and arrived, I don't know, about eleven.

EXT. STATION BARRIER. DAY

VERLOC *hands in the tickets to an official at the barrier and hustles* STEVIE *through.*

INT. BEDROOM IN THE CONTINENTAL HOTEL. NIGHT

VERLOC *hesitates, trying to bring himself to continue. The* ASSISTANT COMMISSIONER*'s shadow passes across him.*

EXT. GREENWICH PARK. DAY

CLOSE *on* VERLOC*'s hand, as he tightens the screw-top on the tin can. This done, he glances at his watch, hands the can to* STEVIE, *gives him an encouraging smile and watches, as* STEVIE *sets off in the direction of the Observatory, the can bouncing against his thigh.* VERLOC*'s umbrella stands propped against a nearby tree.*

VERLOC: (*Voice-over*) In the park, I primed the bomb and sent him off with it.

INT. BEDROOM IN THE CONTINENTAL HOTEL. NIGHT

VERLOC *looks up, his expression suddenly sick with remorse.*

VERLOC: I was fond of him, you know; I was really fond of that boy.

ASST COMMISSIONER: I'm sorry.

(*This is all working out better than the* ASSISTANT

COMMISSIONER *had dared to hope; he looks around now, concerned to lighten the atmosphere.*)

Appalling place you've brought me to.

VERLOC: Serves very well for the refugees they send me over from the Continent. I suppose it's a question of what you're used to.

(*The* ASSISTANT COMMISSIONER*'s expression hardens. He settles, perching on the end of the bed.*)

ASST COMMISSIONER: All right: let's get down to business, shall we?

INT. SHOP. NIGHT

WINNIE *is still behind the counter;* HEAT*'s interrogation is beginning to wear her down and make her feel obscurely troubled.* HEAT, *on the other hand, is in his element.*

HEAT: You see, it strikes me, Mrs Verloc, you probably know more about this bomb business than you're aware of.

WINNIE: What bomb business? I don't know what you're talking about.

(HEAT *considers her for a moment, with stony scepticism. Then he decides to state the facts, coldly and bluntly.*)

HEAT: Bomb went off this morning in Greenwich Park. By accident most like, since one of the perpetrators was blown to bits. And I have reason to suppose your husband might be able to help me with my enquiries, that's all.

WINNIE: Adolf'd never get mixed up in anything like this.

HEAT: I know that; it's just information I'm after. You're sure he hasn't spoken to you about it?

(WINNIE *shakes her head from side to side: there's something about all this which is starting to get to her. There's a silence, during which* HEAT *decides to change tack. He pulls a rolled-up copy of the* Sporting Life *out of his pocket, unfurls it on the counter, smoothes out its pink pages, then, from another pocket, produces a tattered square of cloth and bangs it down on top of the newspaper.*)

I take it you can identify this?

(WINNIE *reaches out for the piece of cloth, real fear in her eyes.*)

(INSET: *on the square of cloth is written in purple marking ink*:)

I AM STEVIE
I LIVE AT 32, BRETT ST
LONDON, W.1

(WINNIE *looks up at* HEAT*; her answer, when it comes, is almost inaudible.*)

WINNIE: Yes.

HEAT: Your brother, is he in the habit of going about labelled?

WINNIE: He sometimes gets a bit confused. So I made that label and sewed it in for him. He's all right, there's nothing wrong with him, it's just sometimes he goes and sees his mother on his own, and I like to be on the safe side . . .

(HEAT *reaches out and takes the label back from her; he returns it to his pocket.*)

HEAT: Is he a short, stocky fellow?

WINNIE: No, he's tall and fair.

(HEAT *nods, his mind racing.* WINNIE *is still frowning, perplexed and worried.*)

I don't understand, that label, whatever'd you tear it out for?

(*The ensuing silence is broken by the clang of the bell on the shop door, which makes them both jump.* VERLOC *stands in the doorway. He seems neither pleased nor suprised to see* HEAT.)

VERLOC: What do you want?

HEAT: A word or two.

VERLOC: Better come upstairs, then.

(*He closes the door behind him and plods across the shop, not looking at* WINNIE. HEAT *falls in behind him and follows him up the stairs.*

The camera stays on WINNIE*: she's desperately trying to make sense of the information offered to her, without much success, judging from the depth of her frown. Suddenly, she jumps up, comes round the counter and moves swiftly and silently over to the stairs.*

HEAT*'s* VOICE *is audible from the room above.*)

HEAT: (*Off-screen*) Took a little while for the penny to drop . . .

INT. SITTING-ROOM. NIGHT

HEAT *follows* VERLOC, *as he crosses to the fire.*

HEAT: It was only when I was talking to your wife just now . . .

INT. STAIRCASE. NIGHT

WINNIE*'s moving silently up the stairs.*

HEAT: (*Off-screen*) . . . I realized you must be the other man.

VERLOC: (*Off-screen*) Are you going to take me in?

INT. SITTING-ROOM. NIGHT

HEAT: I know who you've just been talking to. It's his case now.

(*He plumps himself down at one end of the sofa.*)

But I'm the one who traced you, make no mistake about that.

VERLOC: How?

(HEAT *produces the label from his overcoat pocket.*)

HEAT: Take a look at this.

(*As* VERLOC *does so, the camera pans slowly across the floor to reveal, through the bannisters,* WINNIE *tensely listening below.*)

VERLOC: (*Off-screen*) What's she want to try a dodge like that for?

(HEAT *doesn't answer, instead he speaks with an edge of bitterness.*)

HEAT: (*Off-screen*) Made you an offer, did he?

(VERLOC, *sighing, drops down next to* HEAT *on the sofa.*)

VERLOC: He says if I co-operate fully, I'll get two years maximum.

HEAT: Promises are easy. If I was you, I wouldn't trust him as far as I could throw him.

VERLOC: I got to trust somebody.

INT. STAIRCASE. NIGHT

WINNIE *is listening so hard, her head is straining forward. Her face moves slowly upwards, into a band of reflected light, her dread rising.*

HEAT: (*Off-screen*) So, what are you going to tell them?

VERLOC: (*Off-screen*) Everything.

INT. SITTING-ROOM. NIGHT

VERLOC *looks up at* HEAT, *all barriers down.*

VERLOC: You know me, I'm always straight. That's why I've been so useful to you.

HEAT: Lot of useful things this is going to put a stop to.

(*He looks away, reflecting, his expression grim.*

CLOSE *on* VERLOC.)

VERLOC: See: he was simple.

INT. STAIRCASE. NIGHT

WINNIE *gasps, her head jerks up in shock, she covers her mouth.*

VERLOC: (*Off-screen*) That was the trouble. We went over it all I don't know how many times. Couldn't have been easier. I was just standing there, waiting.

EXT. GREENWICH PARK. DAY

VERLOC *stands waiting, back to camera, the Observatory in the distance. Suddenly, there's an explosion and a column of dark smoke.*

VERLOC*'s horrified reaction is instantaneous.*

As birds rise above the dissipating smoke, VERLOC *turns and runs for dear life.*

EXT. PATHWAY OUTSIDE GREENWICH PARK. DAY

VERLOC *bursts through the gateway and clatters off down the*

deserted thoroughfare, his boots clumping on the earth in the silence left by the explosion.

INT. SITTING-ROOM. NIGHT

There's the shadow of a grim smile on HEAT*'s face.*

HEAT: Then you heard the bang.

INT. STAIRCASE. NIGHT

WINNIE*'s eyes are lit by a stripe of light: they're wide and staring.*

INT. SITTING-ROOM. NIGHT

CLOSE *on* VERLOC.

VERLOC: Came too soon, you see.

INT. STAIRCASE. NIGHT

WINNIE *hand goes up to her cheek: she's transfixed with horror.*

VERLOC: (*Off-screen*) That's when I knew he was gone.

(WINNIE*'s head snaps back, hitting the wall with an audible thud.*)

INT. SITTING-ROOM. NIGHT

VERLOC *shakes his head, his eyes full of a genuine sadness.*

VERLOC: I don't know what could have happened.

EXT. GREENWICH PARK. DAY

STEVIE *saunters up the hill, carrying the bright varnish can, a contented smile on his face, his white handkerchief clutched in his other hand.*

HEAT: (*Voice-over*)We were able to piece it together, more or less. Looks like he stumbled over a root.

(*And, indeed,* STEVIE*'s highly polished boot catches on a gnarled, raised root, and he starts to pitch forward, his hand not going out to break his fall, but across his chest to protect the bomb.*)

INT. SITTING-ROOM. NIGHT

VERLOC *is listening in horror, as* HEAT *talks imperturbably on.*

HEAT: And you're right about him being gone. His head and feet were still there.

INT. STAIRCASE. NIGHT

WINNIE *is in the same position, rigid with fear and grief.*

HEAT: (*Off-screen*) But the rest of him they had to scrape up with a shovel.

(WINNIE*'s hands fly up to cover her ears.*

The stairs, strangely tilted and distorted, from WINNIE*'s* POV, *as she stumbles away, down towards the shop.*)

INT. SHOP. NIGHT

WINNIE*'s* POV, *as she staggers aimlessly towards the counter and lurches round it.*

ANOTHER ANGLE *shows* WINNIE *arriving behind the counter, suddenly grasping the copy of the* Sporting Life, *ripping it in half and hurling it to the floor. Then she sinks back into the chair behind the counter.*

WINNIE*'s* POV: *the shop, with its ugly disposition of ludicrous, bizarre and obscene objects.*

WINNIE *stares blindly out from behind the counter.*

WINNIE*'s* POV *again: her hands come into frame. Her right hand moves across and begins playing with the gold wedding-ring on her left hand. It glitters as it catches the light.*

INT. SITTING-ROOM. NIGHT

VERLOC *leans forward to speak confidentially to* HEAT.

VERLOC: Can't you take me in tonight? I'll come quietly.

HEAT: I daresay. But by tomorrow morning this isn't going to be my case any more, thanks to your new friend.

VERLOC: Jail's the only safe place for me. They'll all be after me now; if I'm not careful, I'm liable to end up with a knife in my back.

(HEAT *considers him for a few seconds; then, he leans forward in his turn.*)

HEAT: You want my advice? Private advice from private citizen Heat?

VERLOC: I do.

HEAT: Clear out. Vanish. We won't chase after you. I can see to that.

(VERLOC *reflects; his hat is still on the back of his head, he's wearing his overcoat and his forehead is slightly beaded with sweat.)*

And neither will your people. They all think you're dead already.

VERLOC: How do you know?

HEAT: I'd say they'd make a logical assumption that it was your guts spread all over Greenwich Park. Wouldn't you?

(This is a new thought for VERLOC*; and* HEAT *decides to leave him with it. He rises to his feet, claps* VERLOC *jovially on the shoulder and walks briskly to the stairs.)*

INT. STAIRCASE. NIGHT

HEAT *descends the stairs, moving at a clip.*

INT. SHOP. NIGHT

HEAT*'s* POV: WINNIE *is still sitting behind the counter, one hand on either side of her face, staring out into space.*

HEAT *looks at her as he approaches: but she doesn't react to his presence in any way and he decides not to speak to her. Instead, he hurries past and out of the shop.*

The bell jerks and trembles on its curved ribbon of steel, jangling harshly.

WINNIE *continues to stare, seemingly entirely unaware of the sound of the bell.*

EXT. STREET. NIGHT

As before, STEVIE *shepherds* WINNIE *towards the bus, in the pouring rain.*

STEVIE: He's a good man, Mr Verloc.

INT. SHOP. NIGHT

WINNIE*'s head drops; she sits there, lost in her memories.*

INT. SITTING-ROOM. NIGHT

VERLOC *stands, gnawing at his thumb, uncertain of how to proceed. Then he catches sight of the food, which is still laid out on the table. He jerks into action, hurries over, hacks himself a piece of bread, then picks up the carving knife and cuts off a thick slab of pink beef.*

He picks the beef up with greasy fingers, flops it down on the bread which he folds and raises to his mouth.

CLOSE *on* VERLOC*'s mouth as it ingests a wayward hunk of beef.*

INT. SHOP. NIGHT

WINNIE*'s hands have moved now, to cover her face: otherwise she hasn't stirred. Nor does she, when* VERLOC *comes stumping down the stairs and into the shop. He stands in front of her for a long moment.*

VERLOC: I never meant any harm to come to the boy, you know that.

(WINNIE *doesn't react in any way.* VERLOC *waits, then tries another tack.*)

I couldn't think how I was going to break it to you. I sat for hours in the Cheshire Cheese, worrying my head off.

(*A slight groan is* WINNIE*'s only response:* VERLOC *takes a maturely philosophical tone.*)

Can't be helped, Winnie, what's done can't be undone.

(WINNIE*'s shoulders begin to shake; for a moment, it's almost as if she's laughing.* VERLOC *takes a step towards her, rattled.*)

You might look at a fellow.

WINNIE: I never want to look at you again, as long as I live.

(*She's said this quite suddenly, through her hands, taking* VERLOC *by surprise.*)

VERLOC: Eh? What?

(*No response.* VERLOC *decides the moment has come for a kindly firmness.*)

Come on, Winnie, be reasonable: this won't bring him back. And suppose it had been me you'd lost, then where would you be?

(*By this time he's reached her; and now he takes her wrists and tries to pry her hands away from her face. This doesn't work: instead, her whole body sways forward out of the chair, so that he has an ungainly struggle to stop her from overbalancing altogether. This enables her to slip free of him, dart across the shop and up the stairs, while he's still finding his feet. He sighs heavily, momentarily at a loss. Then he crosses to the street door, locks it and pulls down the canvas blind. Finally he goes back behind the counter to turn out the gas-lamp.*)

INT. SITTING-ROOM. NIGHT

WINNIE *is sitting at the table now, her head resting on her arms. She doesn't stir at the heavy tread of* VERLOC *coming up the stairs or look at him when he appears. By now, he's worked out another approach.*

VERLOC: You know I don't like to worry you, so I didn't tell you what a spot that Embassy bastard put me in. Eleven years I've been working for them and I risked my life I don't know how many times. There's scores of those revolutionists I've sent off to be caught red-handed and some of the highest in the world have got me to thank for still walking on their two legs. And then this new swine turns up, ignorant, overbearing, thinks he knows it all. I should have taken him by the throat and rammed his head up the Embassy chimney.

(*He picks up the carving knife, hacks off another piece of beef and sticks it directly into his mouth.*)

Sorry, I haven't eaten all day.

(*He's spoken with his mouth full. He swallows the beef and returns to his theme.*)

I could have done, too, they'd never have dared call the police, you know what I mean?

(WINNIE *ignores him completely: he looks down at her, perplexed and discouraged. She lies there, her head resting on her forearm.*

WINNIE*'s* POV*: the room, sideways on.*)

EXT. BRETT STREET. DAY

Outside the shop: as before, STEVIE*, his expression serious and tender, takes* WINNIE*'s face between his hands.*

STEVIE: I love you, Winn.

INT. SITTING-ROOM. NIGHT

WINNIE*, motionless, stares into the middle distance.*

VERLOC *is beginning to lose his patience.*

VERLOC: You're going to have to pull yourself together sooner or later, my girl.

(WINNIE *doesn't react.*)

Perhaps you'd better go up to bed.

INT./EXT. BRETT STREET, DAY

WINNIE *watches* STEVIE *and* VERLOC, *setting off down the street in their bowler hats.*

VERLOC: (*Voice-over*) What you need is a good cry.

INT. SITTING-ROOM. NIGHT

WINNIE *sits up and turns to look at* VERLOC, *speaks very quietly.*

WINNIE: I thought you were like father and son.

VERLOC: What's that?

WINNIE: But you were just taking him away from me to murder him.

VERLOC: Here, hang on a minute . . .

WINNIE: And there was I, sure you'd come home with a cold.

VERLOC: No, I was upset. I was upset about you.

(*She's looking straight at him: he falters and avoids her gaze, mumbling shamefacedly.*)

And the boy, of course.

(VERLOC *makes an effort to strike out in a more constructive direction.*)

Listen, Winnie, we're going to have to make some plans, you understand what I'm saying? I'm going to have to get away, and you're going to need to be extra careful. They'll be keeping a watch on you all the time. You're going to be on your own for a while, till the right moment, then you can slip away and join me.

WINNIE: Abroad?

VERLOC: Well, of course, abroad. I don't want to make it easy for them to catch up with me and do me in, I think too much of you for that.

WINNIE: What about Stevie?

(VERLOC *is shocked into silence; and when* WINNIE *realizes what she's said, she springs to her feet and hurries across the room.*)

VERLOC: Where you going, upstairs?

(*By this time, she's already disappeared up the stairs.* VERLOC *stays where he is, calling up the stairs after her.*)

That's right. Bit of rest and quiet. Won't be long before I join you.

EXT. BEDROOM WINDOW. NIGHT

WINNIE *stands, framed in the window, staring out into the night.*

INT. BEDROOM. NIGHT

WINNIE *has already started packing: her old portmanteau stands open on the bed. She completes the process, then, after a moment's hesitation, she returns to open the third drawer down. She takes out the coloured ball, the musical bear and several pages covered in perfect circles and carries them over to the bed. The bear tinkles randomly as she drops it in the case.*

INT. SITTING-ROOM. NIGHT

VERLOC *sits at the table, munching a beef sandwich. He looks up as he hears* WINNIE*'s footsteps moving to and fro above.*

INT. BEDROOM. NIGHT

HIGH ANGLE. WINNIE *moves up and down, whimpering, wringing her hands. Finally, she reaches a decision and begins to unbutton her dress.*

INT. SITTING-ROOM. NIGHT

VERLOC *looks up in surprise as* WINNIE *appears in her outdoor clothes, complete with hat and black veil, holding a suitcase. He shakes his head again, doing his best to conceal his exasperation.*

VERLOC: Look at the time, Winnie. Your mother'll be in bed before you get there. Show a bit of sense.

(WINNIE *puts the case down and perches on a straight-backed chair.*)

I don't want to make a thing of it, but it was you brought the police here, sewing in that label without telling me. Now take your hat off, I can't do without you this evening.

(*No response from* WINNIE: *she sits up straight, quite motionless, mysterious behind her veil.* VERLOC, *provoked, suddenly lumbers across the room towards her.*)

Come on, take the damn thing off!

(*He reaches out and drags the veil aside, revealing a completely expressionless* WINNIE.)

That's more like it.

(*He retreats again, pacing around the room.*)

The boy's gone. You think I wanted him to blow himself up? It was an accident. Just as much as if he'd been run over by a bus.
(*He moves around in silence for a while, then starts again, goaded by her refusal to respond.*)
You're the one kept pushing him my way, telling me to take him out for walks and that. If you look at it that way, you're as responsible for his death as I am.
(*Her head jerks around to look at him, her first reaction of any kind. Suddenly, he's exhausted; he arrives at the sofa and flops down on it full-length, with a weary groan.*)
I wish to goodness I'd never set eyes on Greenwich Park.
(WINNIE *stares ahead, her back to the table, her veil hanging ragged against her cheek. She closes her eyes.*)

EXT. GREENWICH PARK. DAY

As before, STEVIE*'s boot catches on a raised root and he pitches forward. He clutches the bomb to him protectively. There's a huge explosion. As the smoke slowly clears, the Observatory is seen above, mockingly intact on the skyline.*

INT. SITTING-ROOM. NIGHT

WINNIE*'s eyes are still closed.*

VERLOC *looks across at her: from his* POV *on the sofa, she sits sideways on, motionless.*

VERLOC: Winnie.

EXT. GREENWICH PARK. DAY

STEVIE*'s head has lodged in a fork of the oak-tree: it stares out with a puzzled expression.*

INT. SITTING-ROOM. NIGHT

WINNIE *opens her eyes.*

VERLOC: Winnie.

WINNIE: Yes.

VERLOC: I know what'd do you good.

(*She looks at him, stretched out on the sofa: he's spoken with a strange, throaty intonation.*)

Come here.

(WINNIE *rises, her back to the table. She reaches behind her and picks up the carving knife. Then she crosses the room, the knife concealed behind her back.*

VERLOC *is looking up at her, his expression lascivious. As she leans over him, his hand comes up to caress her cheek and breast.*

A kind of twisted smile contorts WINNIE*'s features. She stoops to plant a kiss on* VERLOC*'s lips and undoes the top button of his waistcoat.*

WINNIE *straightens up: she brings the knife from behind her back and places it carefully against* VERLOC*'s chest. He finally understands what she means to do.*)

Don't.

(WINNIE *plunges the knife into his chest. Then she steps back.*

VERLOC, *the bone knife-handle protruding from his chest, his bowler hat still perched on his head, struggles to his feet. He begins to advance towards* WINNIE, *his hand reaching out to her. She moves slowly backwards, keeping just out of his reach. As he approaches the top of the stairs, he suddenly staggers and crumples, landing full-length on his back. She looks down at him, her expression suffused with hatred.*)

WINNIE: I never wanted you. All I ever wanted was somewhere safe for Stevie.

VERLOC: What?

(VERLOC*'s body convulses as he dies. The spasm dislodges his hat.)*

INT. STAIRCASE. NIGHT

VERLOC*'s bowler goes bouncing down the stairs, all the way to the bottom, where, for a moment, it rocks from one side to another on its brim.*

EXT. TOP DECK OF A CHANNEL STEAMER. DAWN

The camera contemplates WINNIE*, alone on the top deck, impenetrable behind her veil. After a while, she looks down at her wedding-ring. It's difficult to ease off her finger, but she eventually manages it and lays the ring down beside her on the wooden bench. Then she rises and begins to move towards the rail. The camera follows, but she outpaces it; and by the time it arrives at the rail, she's disappeared, and there's only the pearl-grey sea, the pink and yellow fingers of dawn, the deserted deck, the flapping canvas and finally, as the camera completes its circle, the abandoned ring.*

INT. SILENUS RESTAURANT. DAY

The mechanical piano is grinding out some hideously cheerful number, its keys flashing like a mouthful of false teeth.

OSSIPON *sits on his own, a tumbler of brandy at his elbow, his expression melancholy. In his hand is a much-thumbed newspaper cutting. The headline reads: 'Mysterious Suicide of a Lady Passenger from a Cross-Channel Boat.'*

DISSOLVE

EXT. BRETT STREET. NIGHT

WINNIE *is running down the street, as fast as she can, away from the shop. It's foggy and there's a kind of hazy drizzle, giving every street-lamp its halo of mist.* WINNIE *runs blindly on: until suddenly she cannons into a substantial figure. She gasps in shock and looks up to see the robust anarchist,* ALEXANDER OSSIPON, *known to his special friends as Tom.*

WINNIE: Mr Ossipon!

OSSIPON: Mrs Verloc!

(*She straightens up and draws back her veil, looking up at him.*)

WINNIE: You recognized me.

OSSIPON: Of course I did. As a matter of fact, I was on my way to see you.

WINNIE: You were?

(WINNIE *slips her hand under his arm.* OSSIPON *is somewhat taken aback by the course of events but, never one to look a gift horse in the mouth, he allows himself to be drawn along by* WINNIE.)

OSSIPON: Where are we going?

WINNIE: Will you help me?

INT. SILENUS RESTAURANT. DAY

OSSIPON *sits, blearily remembering.*

WINNIE: (*Voice-over*) Can't you take me away? Out of the country tonight?

EXT. BRETT PLACE. NIGHT

They've arrived now in Brett Place, a cramped triangular area, penned in by narrow, terraced houses. They've come to a stop in the gauzy circle of light at the foot of a lamppost. OSSIPON *is cudgelling his brains, furiously calculating how best to take advantage of his windfall.*

OSSIPON: I don't think there's a train till the morning.

WINNIE: Isn't there somewhere you can hide me?

OSSIPON: I can't take you back to my lodgings.

WINNIE: Somewhere else, then?

OSSIPON: It's all very well, but I've hardly any money on me. We anarchists are never very rich.

WINNIE: I have money.

OSSIPON: How much?

WINNIE: All the money.

OSSIPON: What do you mean?

WINNIE: All the money he had in the bank.

(*In the ensuing silence, she leans forward once again, resting her face against his chest. His arms close around her; his expression is blissful.*)

OSSIPON: Then we are saved.

INT. SILENUS RESTAURANT. DAY

A shadow falls across OSSIPON, *interrupting his reverie: the* PROFESSOR*'s harsh voice reveals the shadow's identity.*

PROFESSOR: What's the matter with you?

(*The* PROFESSOR, *holding his glass of beer, sits at the table opposite* OSSIPON, *who's doing his best to reassemble his features, having swiftly pocketed the cutting.*)

I don't understand why you look so morose, I'd heard you'd come into a little legacy.

OSSIPON: Do you want it?

PROFESSOR: What?

OSSIPON: The legacy. You can have it. All of it.

(*The* PROFESSOR *contemplates* OSSIPON *for a moment with some surprise; then he gives a thin smile.*)

PROFESSOR: I shall send off tomorrow for certain chemicals. Things I need. Then, if it's all right, I shall pass you the bill.

OSSIPON: Whatever you like.

(*He empties the tumbler of brandy.*)

(*Voice-over*) Wait a minute: there is a midnight ferry from Southampton to St Malo.

EXT. BRETT PLACE. NIGHT

WINNIE *is looking eagerly up at* OSSIPON.

OSSIPON: Ten-thirty from Waterloo, I think.

WINNIE: Can we go back to the shop?

OSSIPON: What for?

WINNIE: I packed a case.

(OSSIPON *frowns for a second, considering.*)

OSSIPON: Well, all right.

(*They move away from the lamppost, arm in arm.*)

INT. SHOP. NIGHT

The shop is in darkness, except for the overspill of light which comes down the stairs from the sitting-room above, outlining the curious contours of VERLOC*'s bowler hat. The silhouettes of* WINNIE *and* OSSIPON *pass the window and pause, framed in the open doorway.* WINNIE *more or less pushes* OSSIPON *into the shop.*

WINNIE: It's upstairs on the floor.

(She stays in the doorway as OSSIPON *advances nervously across the shop.)*

INT. STAIRCASE. NIGHT

OSSIPON*'s foot catches the bowler hat and he looks down at it wobbling gently from side to side. He frowns in puzzlement and begins to advance, with great caution and reluctance, up the stairs.*

He's two-thirds of the way up the stairs when his foot slips in a pool of viscous blood, pitching him forward. His face lands within inches of VERLOC*'s and he suddenly becomes aware of the bone handle of the knife sticking out of* VERLOC*'s chest.*

He jerks backward with a great yell and tumbles back down the stairs.

INT. SHOP. NIGHT

As OSSIPON *lands at the foot of the stairs, so* WINNIE *careers into the shop, closing the door behind her and throwing herself to the floor alongside* OSSIPON. *Again, the only light is what filters down from upstairs.*

WINNIE: Policeman. He spotted me.

OSSIPON: What?

(WINNIE *slaps a hand over his mouth. His eyes are wide with terror.)*

EXT. BRETT STREET. NIGHT

A policeman in a raincape hesitates, across the road from the shop. Something has caught his attention. He flashes the light of his dark lantern and sets off across the street.

INT. SHOP. NIGHT

The beam from the dark lantern jolts around the room, illuminating dummies in underwear and a rack of dildos.

WINNIE*'s lips move, within an inch of* OSSIPON*'s ear.*

WINNIE: If he comes in, kill me.

(OSSIPON*'s eyes widen, as the policeman tries the doorhandle.)*

EXT. BRETT STREET. NIGHT

The policeman, reassured, moves off.

INT. SHOP. NIGHT

As the policeman's footsteps die away, WINNIE *still clings tightly to* OSSIPON *on the floor.*

WINNIE: They'd hang me, Tom, I can't bear the thought.

(OSSIPON*'s eyes flash as he looks up the stairs.*)

OSSIPON: Did you do that?

WINNIE: He killed my boy.

(*It takes a moment; then* OSSIPON *understands at last.*)

OSSIPON: My God. It was the degenerate in the park.

WINNIE: My Stevie.

(OSSIPON *moves and frightens himself by setting the bowler hat rocking again.*)

OSSIPON: Is the money upstairs?

WINNIE: No. No, it's on me.

OSSIPON: Then let's get out of here or we'll miss the train.

EXT. HACKNEY TUNNEL. NIGHT

A cab comes clattering up the strange tunnel leading into Waterloo Station, throwing a giant shadow.

EXT. WATERLOO STATION FORECOURT. NIGHT

The cab pulls up at the dropping-off point and OSSIPON *and* WINNIE *scramble out.* OSSIPON *pays the driver and then seizes* WINNIE *by the arm, hurrying her into the station.*

OSSIPON: You'd better let me have the money.

WINNIE: Yes, Tom.

(*She takes the wallet out of her pocket and it vanishes into his, as if by magic. They disappear into the station.*)

EXT. WATERLOO STATION. NIGHT

LONG SHOT. *The station is not very crowded and the fog drifts, hanging in the cathedral-like space.* OSSIPON *and* WINNIE *appear in the distance: he stands her under the clock.*

OSSIPON: Wait here.

INT. TICKET-OFFICE AT WATERLOO. NIGHT

OSSIPON *reaches the head of the queue and takes the wallet out of his pocket. The* CLERK *on the other side of the window looks up.*

CLERK: Yes?

(*But* OSSIPON, *his jaw hanging slack, is staring nonplussed at the thick stack of notes crammed into the wallet.*)

Yes?

(OSSIPON *comes to with a start.*)

INT. SILENUS RESTAURANT. DAY

OSSIPON*'s head is lowered, he looks almost ashamed.*

EXT. WATERLOO STATION. NIGHT

WINNIE *waits patiently beneath the clock, which reads 10:13.* OSSIPON *suddenly materializes out of nowhere, takes her arm and leads her over towards a waiting train, handing her her ticket as he does so.*

OSSIPON: We should keep apart until the train leaves.

(*He opens a carriage door and helps her into the last carriage of the train. Then he slams the door and hurries away.*)

INT. STATION BAR. NIGHT

OSSIPON *empties his glass of brandy and gestures to the barmaid.*

OSSIPON: Another one, please.

(*As she turns away to serve him,* OSSIPON *pulls the rolled-up newspaper out of his pocket. He's appalled to see that it's stained with* VERLOC*'s blood. He pushes it down the bar, away from him, checking to see that no one is watching.*)

EXT. STATION PLATFORM. NIGHT
The clock on this platform reads 10:28.

INT. TRAIN COMPARTMENT. NIGHT
WINNIE*'s watching through the window: now she smiles with relief and presently* OSSIPON *climbs into the compartment.*

OSSIPON: I tipped the guard, so we'll have the compartment to ourselves.

WINNIE: You think of everything.

(*She looks up at him admiringly and submits as he takes her hand and moves her to a corner away from the platform. Then he goes to look out of the window.*)

INT./EXT. PLATFORM. NIGHT
OSSIPON*'s* POV: *the clock reads 10.29.*

INT. TRAIN COMPARTMENT. NIGHT

OSSIPON *turns back to smile reassuringly at* WINNIE.

OSSIPON: Extraordinary boy, that brother of yours.

WINNIE: You were the only one that took any notice of him, Tom. I loved you for it.

(OSSIPON *slides along the wooden bench towards her and lifts the veil from her face.*)

EXT. PLATFORM. NIGHT

The hand on the clock moves to 10.30.

A blast on the engine's steam whistle.

INT. TRAIN COMPARTMENT. NIGHT

OSSIPON *leans in to kiss* WINNIE.

EXT. PLATFORM. NIGHT

The train's wheels begin to revolve as the piston jerks.

INT. TRAIN COMPARTMENT. NIGHT

The movement of the train jolts OSSIPON *and* WINNIE *apart.*

EXT. PLATFORM. NIGHT

The train's wheels begin to gather speed.

INT. TRAIN COMPARTMENT. NIGHT

OSSIPON *slides back across the bench to look out of the window.*

INT./EXT. PLATFORM. NIGHT

OSSIPON*'s* POV*: the clock, still reading 10.30, disappears as the train pulls away.*

INT. TRAIN COMPARTMENT. NIGHT

OSSIPON *turns to look at* WINNIE: *he's racked with indecision.*

EXT. PLATFORM. NIGHT

HIGH ANGLE: *the steam engine, belching smoke as its speed increases.*

INT. TRAIN COMPARTMENT. NIGHT

WINNIE *watches* OSSIPON *trustingly, as he turns, his agitation rising, from the platform to her and back again.*

EXT. PLATFORM. NIGHT

The train, gathering speed, seen from the platform.

INT. TRAIN COMPARTMENT. NIGHT

OSSIPON *rises to his feet and moves towards the door.*

WINNIE *watches him, quite calm.*

OSSIPON *uses the leather belt to lower the window: then he leans out.*

EXT. PLATFORM. NIGHT

OSSIPON*'s* POV*: the end of the platform is rushing towards him.*

INT. TRAIN COMPARTMENT. NIGHT

WINNIE *is still looking up at* OSSIPON: *finally he appears to reach a decision.*

OSSIPON: Safe journey.

(*He reaches out of the window.*)

EXT. PLATFORM. NIGHT

OSSIPON*'s hand comes down and turns the handle on the outside of the door.*

INT. TRAIN COMPARTMENT. NIGHT

WINNIE *gasps, as she understands what* OSSIPON *is about to do.*

And he's gone.

EXT. PLATFORM. NIGHT

OSSIPON *flies out and lands in a heap on the platform. He picks himself up and starts running, disappearing up the steps which lead to a pedestrian bridge at the end of the platform. The train whistle wails.*

INT. TRAIN COMPARTMENT. NIGHT

Slowly, WINNIE *rises to her feet, swaying in the speeding train, utterly stricken.*

SLOW DISSOLVE

INT. SILENUS RESTAURANT. NIGHT

OSSIPON *empties another tumbler of brandy. The* PROFESSOR*'s watching him shrewdly, assessing the change that's taken place in him.*

PROFESSOR: You know, Ossipon, if I didn't know you better, I might conclude you were in the throes of remorse.

(OSSIPON *looks up with such open hurt on his face, the* PROFESSOR *realizes he's hit the target.*)

Pull yourself together. Remorse is for the weak. And weakness is the source of all evil on this earth. The time is coming, and it's going to be sooner rather than later, when this will be understood, by governments as well as by individuals, that there can be no progress and no solutions until you make a rational decision to exterminate the weak.

(*The mechanical piano breaks off, in mid-phrase. The* PROFESSOR *leans forward.*)

I myself have no future: but I am a force.

(*He rises abruptly, puts on his hat and raises his glass.*)

To the destruction of what is.

(*As he drains his beer, the mechanical piano resumes. He puts down his glass and strides away across the restaurant.* OSSIPON, *shaken and dejected, reaches for another glass of cognac.*)

EXT. STREET. DAY

The PROFESSOR *emerges, blinking a little behind his spectacles in the pallid sunlight. He sets off down the street.*

The street is more than usually crowded; and before long, the PROFESSOR *is engulfed in throngs of passers-by. He struggles on, against the tide, his ears turning red as he becomes increasingly overcome with contempt and rage. Those passers-by who glance at him react nervously and try to edge away from the incandescent fury which streams off this otherwise shabby and insignificant figure. Finally, hemmed in so firmly by the crowd, he's unable to continue inching forward. His head comes up, his face an image of concentrated hatred.*

His hand comes out of his left-hand pocket: and he squeezes the indiarubber bulb. At once, the sound, which has risen to an almost intolerable level, cuts out. In the ensuing perfect silence, a thin smile begins to spread across the PROFESSOR*'s wintry features; and there's a* FREEZE-FRAME.

NOSTROMO

UNDERWATER. DAY

The camera travels down through tranquil depths, past shifting columns of light and silvery fronds of seaweed. After a while, it discerns a curious shape on the ocean floor, dark and indistinct, surmounted by a gleaming white sphere.

Gradually, the object on the seabed becomes identifiable: it's a skeleton, sitting up, dressed in the rotting remains of a frock-coat. Two ingots of silver protrude, one from each frayed pocket. Not far off lies a tarnished, pearl-handled revolver.

The grinning skull seems to look upwards at an air-bubble, which we follow on its journey towards the surface of the sea.

EXT. GOLFO PLACIDO. DAY

The camera surfaces not far from the coast of a small island, the Great Isabel, a wedge of volcanic land about a mile long. A ravine runs down to a white beach, where a single gnarled tree stoops over a shallow stream. An image of ethereal tranquillity.

Once this is established, the camera pans to contemplate the rugged coastline.

A caption:

THE PORT OF SULACO
IN THE REPUBLIC OF COSTAGUANA
1892

As the caption fades, a VOICE *begins to speak, the voice of an elderly Englishman, tinged with strain and sadness: it's the voice of* GOULD*'s* FATHER.

GOULD SR: (*Voice-over*) America is ungovernable.

(*A fearsome range of snow-capped peaks towers above the little town; the lower slopes of the mountains are coated irregularly with a belt of tropical jungle, which gives way to a dusty plain dotted with scrub and cactus. In this sheltered bay, the sea maintains an unearthly calm, its surface as smooth and glassy as a mirror.*)

(*Voice-over*) Those who worked for her independence have ploughed the sea.

EXT. JUNGLE. DAY

Dense jungle. The hum of insects and screech of birds are suddenly cut through by the clear, sharp sound of a machete slicing through wood. A branch falls away to reveal a young man, a magnificent specimen in his late twenties, who wears a red sweatband around his thick, curly hair. His once white undershirt is stained with oil; and there's a silver whistle round his neck. This is the Italian foreman of the Sulaco docks, known as NOSTROMO.

Another blow of the machete allows us to see his companion, a contrastingly pale Englishman of about thirty, with a determined set to his jaw and piercing eyes: CHARLES GOULD.

GOULD SR: (*Voice-over*) My boy, I don't suppose you remember the legend of the lost treasure of Azuera.

(NOSTROMO *and* GOULD *push on through the undergrowth.*)

EXT. LOWER WORKINGS OF THE SAN TOMÉ MINE. DAY

NOSTROMO *pushes open a rusted gate and beckons* GOULD *forward with an encouraging grin. But* GOULD *has an uncharacteristic moment of hesitation.*

NOSTROMO: Signor Gould.

(GOULD *starts to move forward.*)

GOULD SR: (*Voice-over*) Two sailors, *gringos* of some sort, went up into the mountains to search for some fabulous hoard. They suffered a quite catastrophic fate. They found it.

(GOULD *is through the gate now into a strange, overgrown yard surrounded by collapsed buildings, dotted with the bizarre shapes of abandoned plant and machinery.*)

EXT. ENTRANCE TO THE MINE. DAY

HIGH ANGLE. GOULD *moves through the upper workings of the mine, passing a wagon overturned on its rails, a segment of a great wheel, quilted in moss, vanishing down into the earth. He's moving towards a vast opening, overhung with creepers, obstructed by mounds of rubble, where the rock has collapsed. In his eagerness, he's overtaken* NOSTROMO *now.*

Seen from inside the mine entrance, the ant-like figure of GOULD *stands beneath the immense natural arch of the opening.* NOSTROMO *steps up beside him.*

GOULD: Wait here.

(NOSTROMO *moves over to one side, out of frame.*)

GOULD SR: (*Voice-over*) It fastened on them, wouldn't let them go. It wouldn't even let them die. They became the slaves of the treasure.

(REVERSE SHOT. GOULD *begins to advance into the mine, until he's swallowed up by the darkness, leaving the screen black.*)

EXT. ENTRANCE TO THE CASA GOULD. DAY

The black screen is breached by a rectangle of dazzling light, as a small wooden door, let into one of the massive front doors of the Casa Gould, is opened. A young woman of about twenty-two is briefly silhouetted in the doorway and advances through the tunnel which leads to the patio. This is MRS EMILIA GOULD, *whose frank and open features, generous mouth and truthful eyes are gradually revealed as she moves into* CLOSE-UP.

EXT. PATIO IN THE CASA GOULD. DAY

The central courtyard of the house has an air of years of neglect. Its flagstones are cracked and layered with dust, sprouting tufts of dry grass. In one corner is a coach, a landau, encrusted with cobwebs, leaning dispiritedly forward on its shafts; in another corner is the broad stone staircase, which leads up to a wide verandah, running all the way round the courtyard.

The Goulds' steward, BASILIO, *in his uniform of white linen with a red sash, moves past* MRS GOULD, *as she stands contemplating the patio.*

INT. MINE ENTRANCE. DAY

GOULD *moves across a vast, dim chamber, littered with boulders and ruined machinery. He looks up as he crosses an area of light, his attention caught by a distant, echoing cry.*

Above him is a great natural funnel with a broken ladder running up the inside of it. The funnel is open to the sky and above, a condor, crying out again, passes across the opening.

GOULD SR: (*Voice-over*) My dear boy, this is just what has happened to me out here. I am ensnared by just such an eternal curse: the silver mine at San Tomé; what they are pleased to call the Gould Concession.

INT. GRAN SALA IN THE CASA GOULD. DAY

Dust flies as BASILIO *bangs at the iron clasp securing the tall shutters on the French windows. He manages to heave them open and light floods into the grandiose room.* MRS GOULD *stands among heavy furniture shrouded in dust-sheets. The massive chandelier is stuck with candle-ends, the floor-to-ceiling gilt-framed mirrors are grimed with dust.*

MRS GOULD *crosses to inspect a framed print, a rare interruption to the vast expanse of bare white wall. It shows the workings of the San Tomé mine as a cross-section of the mountain: the above-ground realistically represented on the right; the left side consisting of a warren of tunnels and shafts and underground chambers. The camera closes in on one of the tunnels.*

INT. TUNNEL IN THE MINE. DAY

GOULD *is now deep in the mine. He carries a lantern, which throws distorted shadows on to the slippery walls, stooping as the ceiling gets lower.*

GOULD SR: (*Voice-over*) This is why I sent you back to school in England, away from the bloodshed and crime of this pitiless continent.

EXT. MINE ENTRANCE. DAY

NOSTROMO *has lit a cheroot. He strolls over to the edge of the cliff where a partially-collapsed chute leads down through the jungle. He picks up a nearby rock, rolls it down the chute and listens to its receding clatter. Then he draws on his cheroot, looking down at the little port and the flat sea far below.*

INT. MINESHAFT. DAY

GOULD *is almost bent double, crawling along a shaft shored up with rickety-looking timbers.*

GOULD SR: (*Voice-over*) The only consolation of my old age is the knowledge that you will never set eyes on this poisoned inheritance, safe with your new bride at the far end of the world. As ever, your loving father.

(*There's a whisper of falling dust; and then, startling* GOULD *into immobility, a strange, deep, grinding sound, reverberating awesomely through the bowels of the mine. He waits for a moment. Silence. He decides to press on.*)

INT. CASA GOULD. DAY

The camera follows MRS GOULD *as she advances down the dark and gloomy corridor, which runs the length of the top floor of the house. The train of her dress raises little eddies of dust in her wake. She stops and pushes open a door with some difficulty.*

INT. BEDROOM IN THE CASA GOULD. DAY

MRS GOULD *enters the shuttered room, which is to become her bedroom. She approaches the large four-poster bed and reaches out to feel the open-work lace coverlet. As she touches it, the whole bed lurches away from her: one of its legs has been eaten through by termites.* MRS GOULD *hurriedly withdraws her hand, her expression startled.*

INT. ROCKFACE. DAY

GOULD *turns off the main shaft into a small chamber. He raises his lantern, moves its beam across the rockface. He catches sight of something, steadies the lantern and edges forward, his eyes shining.*

What he's seen is the silver lode: slate grey stone enclosing porphyry strips, which, in turn, contain bright veins of silver set in whitish stripes of asbestos. He reaches out a hand to caress the sparkling threads of silver.

CLOSE *on his face, oddly illuminated by the lantern: he looks like a man in love.*

Suddenly, he's distracted from this by a rumbling roar from much nearer at hand than before. He looks away; and as dust begins to pour into the chamber, he hurries out of it.

INT. MINESHAFT. DAY

There's been a cave-in and GOULD *moves through the swirling dust, only to find his way has been blocked.*

EXT. ENTRANCE TO THE MINE. DAY

As a fine dust begins to drift out of the entrance, NOSTROMO *is already running into the great, gaping mouth of the mine.*

INT. MINESHAFT. DAY

NOSTROMO *arrives on the other side of the cave-in, in a hardly penetrable darkness; and shouts out at the top of his voice.*

NOSTROMO: Signor! Are you there?
A barely decipherable cry signifies GOULD*'s answer. Swiftly, largely by feel,* NOSTROMO *starts shifting rubble, until he finds a way through, up towards the top of the shaft. As he pulls aside a rock and the dust settles, the feeble rays of* GOULD*'s lantern show through a small opening.*

There's an ominous cracking sound and NOSTROMO *looks over his shoulder. Behind him, one of the support timbers is bulging alarmingly. He turns back to scrabble at the gap even more urgently.*

Soon, there's enough of an opening for GOULD *to hand through his lantern so that they can both see what they're doing; and eventually the gap is almost large enough for him to crawl through. Suddenly, however, the suspect timber cracks again and* NOSTROMO *abandons what he's doing and hurries towards it. The whole shaft is low enough for this tall man to wedge his shoulder against the timber.*

GOULD *wriggles his way through the hole he and* NOSTROMO *have made. He grabs the lantern, aware of the urgency of the situation, as once again the timbers groan and crack. He ducks past* NOSTROMO*, who lets him get a good way ahead before he makes a run for it himself. Behind them, the entire passageway caves in in a thunder of crashing rock and dust.*

EXT. ENTRANCE TO THE MINE. DAY

NOSTROMO *and* GOULD *emerge into the bright daylight pursued by a nimbus of dust. They slap at themselves and shake their heads, producing clouds more dust.* GOULD *stops first, looking across at* NOSTROMO.

GOULD: Well, thank you, Nostromo.

NOSTROMO: *Prego.*

(GOULD *smiles and half-turns and they begin to descend, moving down the slope away from the cavernous opening to the mine.*)

EXT. JUNGLE. DAY

Lower down, where the trees begin to thin out, the two men approach the spot where their horses are tethered. Over this, a conversation begins between the GOULDS:

MRS GOULD: (*Voice-over*) Why Nostromo?

GOULD: (*Voice-over*) Apparently, as I expect you know, it's the Italian for bo'sun. Which is what he was.

(NOSTROMO *untethers his silver-grey mare and swings up into the saddle.*)

EXT. COASTAL PLAIN. DAY

CLOSE *on a gnarled pillar of cactus with yellow needles and flowers like an open mouth.* PULL BACK *and* PAN *with* NOSTROMO *and* GOULD *as they gallop along the dirt road towards the town through lines of giant cacti.*

MRS GOULD: (*Voice-over*) So he's Italian?

GOULD: (*Voice-over*) Yes. He came ashore a couple of years ago, passing through on a ship from Genoa, took a liking to the place and decided to stay.

EXT. CALLE DE LA CONSTITUCIÓN. DAY

GOULD *reins in his horse outside the imposing bulk of the Casa Gould, the gates of which are now open. The street is quite narrow and the houses facing the Casa are battered but imposing.*

MRS GOULD: (*Voice-over*) And what does he do?

GOULD: (*Voice-over*) He's the foreman of the docks, the *Capataz de Cargadores.* The harbour-master told me he would always do anything in his power to help a fellow European.

(GOULD *has shaken hands with* NOSTROMO *and now turns to ride directly into the Casa Gould.*)

He said he was a man in a thousand.

(NOSTROMO *is alone now. He shakes his head, a little rueful, turns his mare and trots off, back towards the Plaza Mayor.*)

EXT. VERANDAH IN THE CASA GOULD. DAY

GOULD *and* MRS GOULD *sit on the verandah above the patio, the remains of tea on the table between them.*

GOULD: Do you think I should have given him a tip?

MRS GOULD: I would have thought so.

GOULD: He has such a dignified air about him, I didn't like to, somehow. (*He breaks off, dismissing the subject from his mind and looking around him.*) And the house? Will it do?

MRS GOULD: Oh, it'll more than do.

(*She stretches out her hand and he takes it; but there's a melancholy light in his eye.*)

GOULD: I couldn't help thinking of Father, when I was up at the mine.

MRS GOULD: Well, of course.

GOULD: If only he'd grappled with it in an intelligent way. All those letters he sent begging me never to return, but, you see, he never really knew me. (*He stands and raises her also to her feet.*) Come with me.

INT. BEDROOM IN THE CASA GOULD. DAY

GOULD *is at the window: he prises open one of the shutters and an oblique shaft of light falls across the room. He reaches over for* MRS GOULD *and points up through the window.*

GOULD: There's the mine, up there. (*He turns to her, his eyes shining.*) I touched the silver. (*He kisses her; then begins manœuvring her towards the bed.*)

MRS GOULD: I'm not sure how safe it is.

GOULD: I think we can risk it.

(*They stretch out across the bed, buried in each other's arms. After a long kiss, he breaks away and looks at her.*)

Only the mine can bring stability and justice to a place like this. The changes you want to make, the help you hope to bring to the oppressed can only take place against a background of prosperity. That's why money-making is not only justified, it's necessary.

MRS GOULD: Is it?

GOULD: If I didn't think that, I could never have brought myself to defy poor Father's orders.

MRS GOULD: Oh, Charley, I know he'd be proud of you. (*She reaches over to him, running her fingers through his hair.*) I think you've been splendidly disobedient. (*She draws his head down and kisses him on the mouth. He begins to unlace her dress.*)

GOULD: Reopening the mine is going to take a great deal of capital. But I'll find it. I know I will.

INT. HOLROYD'S OFFICE IN SAN FRANCISCO. DAY

A large office on the eleventh floor of a corner building overlooking the Bay. MR HOLROYD, *the great financier, a burly, imposing figure in a silk-faced frock-coat, a man approaching sixty, is on his feet speaking in a clipped, confident tone, presenting an imperious Roman profile to* GOULD.

HOLROYD: There isn't a reason in the world for me to invest in your silver mine and I may say a good many of my business associates here in San Francisco think I must have taken leave of my senses even to contemplate such an idea. (GOULD *faces him, formally dressed, politely attentive, perfectly calm.*)

GOULD: If I weren't convinced it were a sound investment, I should never have troubled you.

HOLROYD: It defeated your father.

GOULD: It killed him.

(HOLROYD *straightens up, surprised by this flat, unemotional statement. He crosses to the window and stands for a moment, looking out over the Bay.*)

But my father was never a practical man. Nor was he a trained mining engineer. And I am, Mr Holroyd.

(*Something about* GOULD*'s tone seems to please* HOLROYD. *He turns back to* GOULD, *entirely focused.*)

HOLROYD: Very well now. Suppose we agree to finance you. There would then be three parties involved: first, the house of Holroyd . . . (*he makes an inclusive gesture, indicating himself and his office*) . . . which is all right; second, Mr Charles Gould, a citizen of Costaguana. Also all right, to all appearances. And third, and this is where we should pause, should we not, the government of Costaguana. How many of those have there been in the last twenty years?

GOULD: Five. No, six.

HOLROYD: Hm. (*He moves restlessly about the room for a moment, then fixes* GOULD *with his gimlet eye.*) So, the question the first party, which is me, is obliged to put to the second party, which is you, is whether you have the strength to take on the third party, which is whatever gang of thieves and ruffians happens at any given moment to be calling itself the government of Costaguana. Do I make myself clear?

GOULD: I see no reason why we shouldn't buy ourselves a co-operative government.

(HOLROYD *contemplates* GOULD *shrewdly for a moment.*)

HOLROYD: You're a real hustler. I like that.

(*He turns back to the window for a moment, lost in thought.* GOULD *waits patiently. Finally,* HOLROYD *turns to him.*)

Don't expect us to be drawn into any large trouble. Rest assured, in such a case, we shall know how to drop you.

GOULD: You may begin sending out the machinery as soon as you like.

(*He's looking evenly at* HOLROYD, *entirely self-possessed.*)

FADE

EXT. BACK STREET IN SULACO. DAY

GOULD *and* MRS GOULD *ride along a dirt road in a decayed quarter of town, where old colonial stucco-fronted houses, once painted in bright pastel colours, now moulder and rot in front of open drains.* GOULD *reins in at the entrance to an arid courtyard, where naked small children play, and asks a question. There's no answer, but when* MRS GOULD *dismounts and speaks gently to a small boy, he points towards the first floor of a house across the courtyard.* MRS GOULD *distributes coins among the children.*

A caption:

EIGHTEEN MONTHS LATER

INT. STAIRCASE. DAY

MRS GOULD *follows* GOULD *up a dingy wooden staircase and waits as he knocks on a half-open door. There's no answer.* GOULD *advances through the door and* MRS GOULD, *looking around her, follows suit.*

INT. DR MONYGHAM'S SURGERY. DAY

The surgery is plain to the point of austerity and, although the plaster on the walls is crumbling, spotlessly clean. But it clearly serves as living-quarters as well as surgery and a rudimentary kitchen is built into one corner, with a wooden table, on which there stands a bowl containing a large water-melon. Considerable numbers of books are stacked vertically against one wall. When GOULD *first enters the room, it appears to be empty: until he notices a pair of feet on the end of a consulting couch, protruding from behind an adjustable screen.* GOULD *approaches the feet cautiously.*

GOULD: Dr Monygham?

(*The owner of the feet grunts interrogatively by way of response.* GOULD *peers round the screen.*)

My name is Gould.

(DR MONYGHAM *is a man of 50, with iron-grey hair and a habitually sardonic expression made fiercer by two deep and irregular scars, one on each cheek. He wears an old flannel shirt with a large check, outside his trousers. He looks up at* GOULD *with profound suspicion.*)

MONYGHAM: I know who you are.

(MRS GOULD*'s face appears around the screen.*)

GOULD: And this is my wife.

(MONYGHAM *is dreadfully disconcerted by the appearance of a woman; he rises abruptly from the couch.*)

MRS GOULD: Please forgive us for intruding on you like this, Doctor.

GOULD: Perhaps you've heard that I am in the process of reopening my father's silver mine . . .

(*He breaks off, taken aback by* MONYGHAM*'s unexpected movement across the room. Because his ankles have been severely damaged, he has a distinctive limp, scuttling nimble and crab-like on his bare feet. He reaches the kitchen area.*)

MONYGHAM: May I offer you some water-melon, Mrs Gould? I'm afraid it's all I have in at the moment.

MRS GOULD: No, thank you.

MONYGHAM: No, I don't care for it much myself: but did you know one will provide all the nourishment you require for three days?

GOULD: Really?

MONYGHAM: Take my word for it.

GOULD: Mining is a dangerous business; and at my wife's suggestion I've had a hospital built up there. I've come to ask you if it would interest you to become our medical director.

MONYGHAM: Not in the least.

(GOULD *stiffens, affronted.*)

GOULD: Well, in that case . . .

MRS GOULD: May I ask why not, Doctor?

MONYGHAM: If you spend long enough failing to help people at their hour of greatest need, you'll find that interest hardly comes into the matter. I can't imagine why you thought of me in the first place.

GOULD: My father spoke of you in his letters.

MONYGHAM: And did he tell you that I am distrusted and cordially disliked by the entire population of Sulaco?

GOULD: He did.

MRS GOULD: But he also said you were an extremely good doctor.

(*She's succeeded in disconcerting him again. He looks at her, fully aware, for the first time, of her forcefulness and charm.*)

And we've discovered it's your practice to treat the poorer families in the town free. So you can't be entirely indifferent to the welfare of your patients.

(*She looks at him, half-stern, half-candid. And he looks away, troubled, unable to hold her clear gaze.*)

INT. INTENDENCIA. DAY

A huge, leather-covered desk top. GOULD*'s shadow falls across it and a small leather pouch, clinking discreetly, is placed at its centre.*

The desk belongs to SEÑOR GAMACHO, *political chief of Sulaco. He sits staring at the pouch, his large face sweat-stained and poorly shaven. Then he looks up at* GOULD, *who stands opposite him, immaculate. From outside in the square drifts up the sound of a military band, massacring some familiar piece of Verdi.*

WIDE SHOT. GAMACHO*'s office is on the first floor of the Intendencia, the town's administrative HQ. It's a palatial room, but despite the chandeliers and French windows and floor-length mirrors, it's still unmistakably shabby and fly-blown.* GAMACHO *tips his chair back on two legs.*

GAMACHO: Of course, the export of precious metals is a matter of the greatest delicacy, Señor Gould.

GOULD: Well, indeed, and this is why it seemed so important to clarify matters with Your Excellency. We shall be ready to begin bringing the silver down before the end of the year. So we greatly appreciate Your Excellency's kind co-operation.

(GAMACHO *hesitates a moment: then, as if on impulse, he reaches for a rubber stamp, stamps some papers and scribbles his initials across the stamp. Then he leans back again, waving a limp hand in the direction of the window.*)

GAMACHO: Ah, Lucia di Lammermoor! I adore Mozart. Do you not?

GOULD: Depends.

(*His manner has become cold and businesslike. He gathers up the papers and then, to* GAMACHO*'s amazement, he loosens the neck of the pouch and pours a quantity of twenty-dollar gold pieces on to the desk. This done, he carefully folds the pouch, pockets it, turns on his heel and strides towards the door.* GAMACHO *watches him, his mouth ajar, outraged by this flouting of the proprieties.*)

EXT. ALBERGO D'ITALIA UNA. DUSK

The Albergo, which proclaims its name in large black letters on a new wooden sign, is one of the oldest houses in the area. It's situated half-way between the town and the harbour and separated from the railway tracks only by an oleander hedge. The upper floor of the two-storey building, which only runs above the central area of the house, is punctuated by strangely ecclesiastical windows, as narrow as slits. It sits, isolated on the plain, lit by the fiery rays of the setting sun.

Suddenly, a man in his sixties wearing a cook's apron erupts backwards into the courtyard of the inn. He's holding a frying-pan, from which arises a column of thick black smoke, and uttering a loud and eloquent volley of oaths in Italian. This is the proprietor, GIORGIO VIOLA, *an impressive figure whose magnificent leonine head is haloed in a cloud of thick white hair. He tips the contents of the pan on the ground; and from corners of the courtyard a number of dogs and a couple of small brown pigs begin to make their way purposefully towards the discarded food. Then, he throws the pan down in an access of rage; and the two Chinese girls who've been watching nervously pick it up and scuttle away. Around the corner comes* NOSTROMO: *he's stripped to the waist with a towel over his shoulder; he's been washing at the water-barrel in the yard. He throws an arm round* VIOLA*'s shoulders. Dialogue in Italian.*

NOSTROMO: It's not good for you to get so angry, old man. Why don't you go in and find me a cigar?

(*Before* VIOLA *can react to this,* MRS GOULD, *on horseback, rides into the courtyard. She dismounts and* NOSTROMO, *quite unselfconscious in his shirtless state, takes the horse's bridle.*)

MRS GOULD: *Buona sera, Giorgio.*

(*Out of politeness,* VIOLA *answers her in English.*)

VIOLA: Signora Gould, this is Signor Fidanza, who lives in our house.

(NOSTROMO *bows politely to* MRS GOULD*; but she holds out her hand for him to shake, her expression full of goodwill, and addresses him in Italian.*)

MRS GOULD: You're the one they call Nostromo. My husband has often spoken of you. How helpful you were when we arrived.

(NOSTROMO *seems pleased and he inclines his head again, modestly acknowledging his own good repute. He speaks to her in Italian.*)

NOSTROMO: Where did you learn such good Italian?

MRS GOULD: My aunt married an Italian gentleman. I spent a lot of time with her in Lucca.

NOSTROMO: Shall I tether your horse?

MRS GOULD: No, I can only stay a moment. (*She turns to* VIOLA.) And how is your wife?

VIOLA: The *padrona* is a little better, Signora. (*He reverts to English.*) Thank you for asking.

(MRS GOULD *now also reverts to English.*)

MRS GOULD: My husband has spoken to the *jefe*: you may have the lease on the inn. It's yours for as long as you want to stay here.

(VIOLA *is momentarily overwhelmed; he grasps her hand and kisses it, speaking, in his excitement, in Italian.*)

VIOLA: Thank you, Signora: this is a great thing for me. (*He turns to* NOSTROMO.) Do you hear that, Gian' Battista? The English lady has won for us our lease.

NOSTROMO: Congratulations, old man.

(MRS GOULD *hands* VIOLA *a little box. Dialogue continues in Italian.*)

MRS GOULD: And here.

(*He opens the box. Inside is a pair of spectacles with silver*

frames. He takes them out, smiling contentedly, and perches them on his nose.)
Now you can read your Bible in the evening.

VIOLA: Signora, you are an angel!

MRS GOULD: And now I must get back. Good day to you both.
(NOSTROMO *holds the horse steady as she swings back up into the saddle.*)

VIOLA: A thousand thanks, Signora.

NOSTROMO: They tell me your husband's mine is ready to open, Signora.

MRS GOULD: End of the month, Signor Fidanza.
(*She rides away: and* VIOLA, *unable to contain his joy any longer, turns to* NOSTROMO *and throws his arms around him, letting off a great whoop of joy.* NOSTROMO *takes his arm and leads him back towards the inn.* VIOLA*'s eyes are bright with happiness.*)

VIOLA: Just one word to the *jefe*, you see. That's all it took.

NOSTROMO: Yes.

VIOLA: This is a great thing.

INT. LIVING-ROOM IN THE ALBERGO. DUSK

VIOLA*'s wife and daughters are in the big ground-floor room which serves as kitchen and living-room in his private quarters.* TERESA, *his wife, is a strikingly handsome woman some twenty years his junior, with raven-black hair. She lies propped up on the day-bed where she spends a good deal of her time, her skin sallow with illness.* LINDA, *his older daughter, is about sixteen, pale, black-haired and intense; she's moving around the room lighting the oil-lamps.* GISELLE *is two years younger than her sister and a complete contrast, fair, lively and mischievous, more delicately beautiful; she's sitting at the table, daydreaming, as* VIOLA *bustles in, followed by* NOSTROMO. *Dialogue in Italian.*

VIOLA: They're fine people, the English.

TERESA: Not you as well: it's bad enough that Gian' Battista runs after them everywhere they go.

VIOLA: Teresa . . .

TERESA: You even took that stupid name they gave you. Nostromo. What sort of a name is that?
(NOSTROMO *seizes the opportunity to go over and kiss* TERESA

on the forehead. He's clearly accustomed to her attacks and not at all put out by them. Meanwhile, VIOLA *is gesticulating in the direction of a sun-faded colour lithograph of Garibaldi in his* bersaglieri *hat with its cock's feathers.*)

VIOLA: You don't know how many Englishmen gave their lives for liberty fighting beside Garibaldi in Uruguay. And when the general went to London, the princesses kissed his hands! It was an Englishman gave me my Bible in Palermo.

TERESA: You're as bad as each other.

(VIOLA *shakes his great mane of hair, at a loss as to how to impress* TERESA *with the importance of what's happened.*)

VIOLA: You don't understand, this is a great thing for me!

INT. FURNACE-ROOM AT THE MINE. DAY

Silence. Black screen. Slowly, diagonally across the screen, flows a trickle of molten metal, smoothly advancing like a fiery snake.

CLOSE *on* GOULD, *his face lit by the glow of the flames, entranced. The stream of liquid silver flows evenly into a rectangular mould.*

EXT. LOWER WORKINGS OF THE MINE. DAY

OVERHEAD SHOT. *The area has been completely transformed. A group of buildings including the furnaces and stamping-mill stands not far away from the restored village, which consists of simple huts with red corrugated iron roofs.*

Some sort of ceremony is obviously in progress. There's the modest sound of a small Indian band, performing on flutes and drums. The San Tomé miners, mostly small, stocky, powerful Indians, with dignified and melancholy faces, stand in formation in their green and white company ponchos. Further off, a roped-off area is crammed with a number of seated, overdressed dignitaries.

A REVERSE SHOT *reveals that this is all seen from the* POV *of* DR MONYGHAM, *standing on the balcony of the new white-frame hospital building, his white housecoat open over his habitual check shirt. He decides he's seen enough and, with an ironic expression, turns and hobbles back into the hospital.*

CLOSER *now on the dignitaries' podium, a number of faces are recognizable: there's* MR HOLROYD, *attended by a couple of featureless men in suits;* GAMACHO; *and the* GOULDS, *formally dressed. And there are also a number of new faces: the plump, bespectacled President-Dictator,* DON VINCENTE RIBIERA, *looking like a university don in a morning coat; the robust-looking, piratical Commander of the local garrison,* GENERAL PABLO BARRIOS, *whose uniform consists of a startlingly grubby blue tunic with a couple of tarnished medals and discoloured white peg-top trousers stuffed into battered red boots, the whole effect nicely set off by a black patch over one eye;* DON JOSÉ AVELLANOS, *a distinguished son of Sulaco, with close-cropped white hair, a strange, wedge-shaped beard and ramrod-straight back; his daughter* ANTONIA, *a strikingly beautiful dark girl in her mid-twenties, dressed austerely in black, black mantilla and a black fan; and* GENERAL MONTERO, *the Minister of War, a sinister, overbearing figure with a harsh Aztec profile, whose uniform is a fantasia in olive green, encrusted with gilt embroidery, plus cumbersome ceremonial sword and a great cocked hat with ostrich plumes.*

Two burly miners, wearing leather skull-caps and carrying between them a strange contraption with long handles, hurry forward towards a plain wooden table set out in front of the dignitaries, shepherded by DON PEPE, *the supervisor of the mine, painfully squeezed into a shiny formal suit. The miners arrive at the table, on which is set out a tray of sawdust, and, on* DON PEPE*'s instructions, with much clanking of machinery, they empty into the tray a freshly-minted and dazzlingly bright silver ingot.*

The distinguished guests crane forward, riveted in their various ways by the appearance of the ingot. GENERAL MONTERO *runs a pink tongue over dry lips.* GOULD *rises to his feet and raises a hand; and the band comes to a ragged halt. A moment of deep silence; and then* GOULD *begins to speak.*

GOULD: This is the first ingot to be forged at the San Tomé mine for twenty years; and I thank you all for the work you've done in helping to produce it. May it signal a return to prosperity and progress! And we would be honoured, Señor President, if you would accept the ingot as our gift.
(RIBIERA *is completely taken by surprise. Fumbling with his spectacles and aware of* MONTERO*'s ferocious glare, he half-rises to his feet.*)

RIBIERA: No, no, Señor Gould . . . perhaps . . . no, please present it to our distinguished visitor, Señor Holroyd.
(*Now, it's* HOLROYD*'s turn to look up. Far more collected than*

RIBIERA, *who's now untidily subsiding back into his seat, he simply drawls without rising.*)

HOLROYD: Give it to the lady.

(*It's clear from his gesture he means* MRS GOULD, *who colours, extremely disconcerted.* GOULD *beckons her forward.*)

GOULD: My dear.

MRS GOULD: Oh, no, Charley, I couldn't.

GOULD: Please.

(MRS GOULD *joins him by the table. She slips off one of her gloves and lays a hand reverently on the surface of the silver.*)

MRS GOULD: It's still warm.

(*They're in a position to be able to murmur to each other without being overheard, except by* DON PEPE: *and* GOULD *leans towards her.*)

GOULD: You must keep it, my dear.

MRS GOULD: Are you sure?

GOULD: Yes: to remind us of our good intentions.

(MRS GOULD *overcomes her uncertainty, picks up the ingot and raises it above her head. The miners break into a spontaneous cheer and, at a signal from* GOULD, *the band resumes.*

LONG SHOT. *Far below, in the valley, the tiny figure of* MRS GOULD, *still holding the ingot aloft.*)

INT. MINE ENTRANCE. DAY

CLOSE *on an imposing centre-piece on a spotless tablecloth on a long table set for a formal luncheon: it consists of a solid silver sculpture representing a relief map of Costaguana.*

A WIDER ANGLE *reveals an extraordinary tableau: the celebratory luncheon has taken place in the entrance to the mine itself, lit by dozens of flaming torches and hundreds of candles. A dais has been built for a small orchestra, which sits silhouetted against an enormous flag of Costaguana, red and yellow stripes with two palm trees in the centre. The President-Dictator is on his feet, drawing to the end of a speech which seems not to have had an enlivening effect on its audience. He stands by his chair, at the centre of the long table, also on a dais; this is the top table, facing out towards the lesser tables below, and our principals are variously disposed along its length:* MRS GOULD, *for example, sits on the President's right; and on her right is a semi-comatose* GENERAL BARRIOS. GENERAL

MONTERO*'s poached eye is fixed obsessively on the silver centre-piece.*

RIBIERA (*Off-screen*) Your beautiful town of Sulaco, cut off as it is by these great mountains, has long slumbered in artificial isolation. But in the few years which separate us from a new century, we are determined to integrate you fully into our nation by building roads, a railway even, through this mighty range. Meanwhile, Don Carlos . . .

(*At one of the tables below is* DR MONYGHAM. MRS GOULD *catches his eye and smiles down at him; but he looks away, embarrassed at having been caught staring at her.*)

. . . my Minister of War, General Montero and I . . .

(MONTERO *shoots him a far from friendly glance.*)

. . . congratulate you on the glorious reopening of your mine. We shall never forget your support, which played so decisive a part in our Presidential campaign.

(*There's a polite ripple of applause, under cover of which* GENERAL BARRIOS *leans towards* MRS GOULD *and observes in a stage whisper:*)

BARRIOS: Take my word for it, señora, your husband has bought himself the best possible man for the job.

(RIBIERA, *meanwhile, raises his glass.*)

RIBIERA: So I would ask you all to join me in a toast:

(*A waiter hovering in the vicinity of* GENERAL BARRIOS *finds himself deftly relieved of his champagne bottle.*)

To our national honour!

(*Everyone stands and gives the toast. The orchestra launches into the national anthem, the usual pompous, sub-Verdian dirge: but when everyone has resumed their seat, it becomes clear that one man is still standing:* GENERAL MONTERO. *He silences the orchestra with a ferocious gesture and looks truculently about him for a moment. He presses his napkin to his champagne-sodden moustache and then discards it on the table; where the white linen shows, quite clearly, the marks of the black dye in his moustache.*)

MONTERO: Ladies and gentlemen: you will not find me on your list of scheduled speakers. But I wish to remind you that our national honour is, now as ever, in the hands of the Army.

(BARRIOS *looks away, disgusted, and empties another glass of champagne.*)

And I should like to propose a toast myself.

(*He turns menacingly towards* HOLROYD, *glowering at him with his beady, domineering stare. Then his hand comes off his sword-hilt to point accusingly at* HOLROYD.)

To you, Mr Yanqui Holroyd. To the man who has brought us four millions and a half of American dollars.

(*It sounds more like a threat than a toast: and as the company struggles uncertainly to its feet again,* BARRIOS *mutters truculently under his breath.*)

BARRIOS: And to you: the man who wishes he could think of a way to steal it.

(*As the orchestra strikes up again and* MONTERO *comes rigidly to attention,* BARRIOS *becomes aware that* MRS GOULD *has overheard him. He winks at her with his single eye.*)

Never trust a man who dyes his moustache.

(MRS GOULD *smiles: but she's genuinely alarmed by the whiff of brimstone in the air.*)

INT. STAMPING-MILL. DAY

There's a far smaller gathering for the final ceremony of the day, just inside the door of the large, plain mill, where the chutes bring the ore in from the mine. The GOULDS, HOLROYD *and his people, the obsequious* GAMACHO, DON JOSÉ AVELLANOS, ANTONIA, *the glowering* GENERAL MONTERO *and* DR MONYGHAM *surround the small, rotund figure of the President-Dictator, who flourishes a large pair of scissors.*

RIBIERA: And it gives me great pleasure to declare the stamping-mill of the San Tomé mine officially open.

EXT. STAMPING-MILL. DAY

As RIBIERA *fumbles with the scissors and cuts the ribbon which stretches in front of him,* GOULD *signals to* DON PEPE, *who throws a couple of switches. Immediately, the ore begins to pour down the renovated chutes; and, a moment later, the giant stamps which crush the ore begin to pound.*

INT. STAMPING-MILL. DAY

Inside, the sound is inconceivably loud; and a spasm of horror crosses RIBIERA*'s face.* MONTERO, *on the other hand, is completely unmoved by the racket; indeed he quite unexpectedly puts his arm around the far shorter* RIBIERA *in a gesture of ominous affability.* GOULD*'s expression, meanwhile, is fiercely exultant; he puts an arm around* MRS GOULD *and begins to escort the party out of the mill door.*

EXT. STAMPING-MILL. DAY

Outside, the sound is scarcely less deafening. As the formal party begins to straggle out into the afternoon sun, the whole valley and the mountains above reverberate with the violent pounding crash of the great stamps. MRS GOULD *slips over to* DR MONYGHAM, *raising her voice against the thunder from the mill.*

MRS GOULD: Have you time to show me around the hospital, Doctor? I'm anxious to see what progress you've made.

MONYGHAM: Follow me.

(*He begins hobbling off towards the hospital at a considerable rate, his expression for once one of unfeigned pleasure.*)

EXT. COASTAL PLAIN. DAY

A procession of closed carriages clatters through the strange forest of cactus at the foot of the mountain in the late afternoon glow.

INT. CARRIAGE. DAY

The occupants of one of the carriages are the GOULDS, MR HOLROYD *and* DR MONYGHAM.

HOLROYD: Well, we've made a strong start. And President Ribiera seems a solid enough citizen. But it is only a start. We need to look into this question of a railway; we need to open a newspaper, how come all the press here seems to hate the President? And I didn't like the cut of that General Montero. Maybe we should think about bringing in some arms, just for defence, you understand.

MRS GOULD: I see you like to be in complete control.

HOLROYD: It can't be helped, Mrs Gould. Soon we'll be giving the word for everything: trade and industry, law, newspapers, art, politics, even religion, from Cape Horn clear up to Smith's Sound. America is going to run the world's business, whether the world likes it or not.

(MONYGHAM *is looking at him with open distaste; he exchanges a glance with* MRS GOULD, *who's trying to conceal her own unease.*)

INT. NOSTROMO'S ROOM IN THE ALBERGO D'ITALIA UNA. EVENING

GISELLE*'s wide-eyed expression is reflected in* NOSTROMO*'s small dressing-table mirror. Then* NOSTROMO*'s reflection comes into frame, as he leans forward, meticulously combing his hair. Gaudy, raucous music from the distant fiesta is carried on the breeze through the open window.* NOSTROMO *becomes aware of* GISELLE *staring at him: his reflection winks and hers blushes. He puts down his comb and stretches out a hand.*

A WIDER ANGLE *reveals how stark and simple* NOSTROMO*'s room is; and also that he is being watched intently by the two girls,* LINDA *and* GISELLE. *Now* LINDA *hurries to fetch a grey hat with silver tassels, which she hands to him. He puts it on, adjusting the angle exactly. His spotless white shirt is tucked into black trousers, with a row of tiny silver buttons down each seam. He wears a red cummerbund and highly-polished black boots with gleaming spurs.*

He rises to his feet and gestures again. This time, both girls rush to get his embroidered leather jacket, notable for the size and splendour of its ornamented silver buttons. GISELLE *gets to it first, but* LINDA *snatches it away from her. She holds it out for* NOSTROMO, *who slips his arms into the sleeves. As he adjusts it and checks its appearance in the mirror,* GISELLE, *speaking in English, murmurs to him in a low, provocative voice.*

GISELLE: Will you be coming back tonight, Gian' Battista?

(LINDA *turns on her sister indignantly and slaps her wrist, blushing furiously.* NOSTROMO *doesn't answer, but it's clear from his reflection that he's amused.*)

EXT. PLAZA MAYOR. NIGHT

The Plaza Mayor, the town's central square, is an enormous space, leading off the Calle de la Constitución. At the far end are the gardens of the Alameda, dry, dusty and neglected, disposed around a disused fountain; one side is dominated by the overbearing façade of the cathedral; another by the baroque excess of the Intendencia; and a third by a colonnaded row of shops and offices.

It's this side along which NOSTROMO, *an extremely striking figure on his silver-grey mare, now rides slowly through the animated crowds.*

Temporary booths have been erected for the sale of sweetmeats, fruit, coconuts and cigars. Groups stand drinking maté from gourds or eating food wrapped in tortillas from earthen pots on open fires. Music blares out from a kind of huge wooden tent-like structure with open sides, erected for the occasion in the Alameda. Couples whirl in wild and unrestrained dance, occasionally staggering out, bathed in sweat and trembling, to lean, panting, against the wooden struts. People point out NOSTROMO *as he passes.*

NOSTROMO *reins in his mare for a moment to study his reflection in the plate-glass window of Anzani's emporium. He's about to move on, contented with what he's seen, when all of a sudden, he's struck in the face by something, which he recovers quickly enough to catch. He opens his hand to reveal a red hibiscus. He looks around, half-puzzled, half-smiling.*

The crowd begins to part and, from NOSTROMO*'s* POV, *we watch the approach of a strikingly attractive mulatto girl:* PAQUITA. *She wears an off-the-shoulder white chemisette, a tight blue skirt and a small golden comb in her hair. He spurs on his mare, mischievously, so she has to hurry to catch up with him.*

Across the square, hurrying through the crowds, following NOSTROMO, *are* LINDA *and* GISELLE. *They arrive at the fringe of the crowd, just as* PAQUITA *draws level with the mare.*

PAQUITA: Why do you pretend not to see me when I pass?

(NOSTROMO *looks at her for a moment, entirely straight-faced.*)

NOSTROMO: Because I don't love you any more.

(*Tears spring to her eyes.* LINDA *and* GISELLE *watch, even more fascinated than the rest of the crowd.*)

PAQUITA: Is that true?

NOSTROMO: No.

(*He reins in the mare and extends a foot, smiling. She takes one of his hands, steps on to his foot and swings up to perch on his knee. He puts a hand round the back of her neck and kisses her on the mouth. Applause from the crowd.*

LINDA *looks down, mysteriously affected;* GISELLE *breaks into an involuntary smile.*

NOSTROMO *stretches out a hand and raises his voice.)*

Give me a knife!

(*A number of men in the crowd hurry forward to oblige him. He reaches out and chooses one of the knives.*)

I had no money to bring you a present for the fiesta. So you may have my best silver buttons.

(*He hands* PAQUITA *the knife. She looks at him, hesitant.*)

Go on.

(PAQUITA *steadies herself, raises the knife and takes hold of one of the buttons.*

CLOSE *on the knife as it starts to saw through the thread.*

LINDA *and* GISELLE *watch, transfixed, as the button comes free and a cheer goes up from the crowd.*

PAQUITA *drops the severed button into* NOSTROMO*'s outstretched hand and begins to cut off another.*

LINDA *comes to herself and tugs at* GISELLE*'s sleeve, but* GISELLE *shakes herself free, determinedly ignoring her sister.*

There's another roar from the crowd as the second button comes off. PAQUITA *drops it into his palm and begins on the third button.*

LINDA*'s watching again, in spite of herself.*

PAQUITA*'s eyes are shining; she's in the grip of erotic excitement.*

GISELLE *watches, as if in a dream.* LINDA *shakes her arm, then starts to drag her struggling sister away through the crowd.*

The last button comes off to more applause. PAQUITA *passes the knife back to its owner and cups her hands so that* NOSTROMO *can pour the buttons into them. She leans forward, her eyes flashing and whispers something to him. A slow smile spreads across his face.*)

EXT. VERANDAH OF THE CASA GOULD. NIGHT

MRS GOULD *lies in a fringed hammock, set up in one corner of the verandah.* GOULD *sits nearby. Two huge flowers of fireworks explode somewhere above the Plaza and random sounds of celebration float up the street. The verandah has been improved by the addition of bunches of flowers and shrubs in large pots against the wrought-iron railings and clusters of* flor de noche buena, *blazing outside the doors to the various reception rooms. It's very late.*

MRS GOULD: He couldn't have been more civil, your Mr Holroyd; but he also seemed exceptionally unimaginative.

GOULD: Nevertheless, he's a considerable man. His name is known to millions of people. His interests are immense, especially in silver and iron.

MRS GOULD: He certainly worships silver and iron. I thought him the most awful materialist.

(GOULD *looks at her for a moment, his expression serious.*)

GOULD: I put my faith in material interests.

(MRS GOULD *frowns, troubled by this, not knowing quite how to respond. Silence, except for the night insects and the distant fiesta. Eventually, her brow clears.*)

MRS GOULD: I love this house.

GOULD: It always used to be rather gloomy. You've given it life, Emilia. (*Silence. He rises to his feet.*) Don't you think it's time we went to bed? It's almost dawn.

MRS GOULD: It can't be, is it?

(*She takes his outstretched hand and swings gracefully down from the hammock.*)

INT. MRS GOULD'S BEDROOM. NIGHT

The bedroom is now transformed into a very feminine domain. The silver ingot sits on an open bureau, holding down a pile of papers. The four-poster bed is fringed with patterned silk.

GOULD *sits next to* MRS GOULD *on the edge of the bed. He turns her face towards him and kisses her. Then, gently, he pushes her back until they're both lying on the bed.*

CLOSE *on* MRS GOULD*'s face as they kiss. Suddenly her eyes open, as the window begins to rattle oddly. She half-turns away, distracted.* GOULD, *however, seems oblivious to the sound, turns her face back to him and kisses her again. She closes her eyes and submits to the embrace.*

CLOSE *on the window, which is still vibrating strangely.*

EXT. SULACO HARBOUR. NIGHT

The dark town, seen from the sea, the mountains looming above and the stars grown pale in the sky. Out here, it becomes clear that the sound, which has caused the windows to rattle, is the distant pounding of the stamping-mill, up at the mine. It grows louder over the image, dully roaring across the dead calm waters of the Gulf, ominous and overbearing.

FADE

EXT. DECK OF A STEAMER. DAY

MARTIN DECOUD *steps tentatively out on to the deck; he's wearing a round hat, but still has to screw up his eyes against the fierce sun. He's a man in his early thirties with a fair beard and moustache, very fashionably dressed. He moves to the edge of the deck and rests a manicured hand on the rail.*

His POV: *the steamer has docked at the quayside in Sulaco and* DECOUD *can see the roofs of the town, the plain beyond, the rearing mountain range.*

A middle-aged couple pause for a moment beside him and the MAN *speaks:*

MAN: Doesn't seem to have changed a bit, does it?

DECOUD: Even smells the same.

(*He's spoken with a characteristic tone of dry irony; and the couple moves on. But a close-up reveals that, to his own surprise, he's suddenly extremely moved to be back in Costaguana. Quite involuntarily, tears spring to his eyes.*)

EXT. QUAYSIDE. DAY

A welcoming committee has turned out to meet the steamer, which, as can now be seen from the tricolore *fluttering at the stern, is French.* DON JOSÉ AVELLANOS *and his daughter* ANTONIA *stand a little apart from the trim figure of* GOULD *and the ramshackle* GENERAL BARRIOS, *whose one eye blinks blearily in the sunshine.*

It's ANTONIA *who first spots* DECOUD *at the rail above; she nudges her father who immediately waves enthusiastically.*

EXT. DECK OF THE STEAMER. DAY

Suddenly aware of AVELLANOS, DECOUD *pulls himself together, raises his hat in acknowledgement of the greeting and reassumes his habitual expression of cool detachment.*

He moves towards the gangplank.

EXT. QUAYSIDE. DAY

At the foot of the gangplank, AVELLANOS *is waiting to enfold* DECOUD *in his arms. He kisses him on both cheeks, clearly powerfully affected;* DECOUD, *by contrast, is now entirely calm.*

AVELLANOS: I knew you would want to supervise everything personally.

(DECOUD *nods, but his eye is on* ANTONIA, *who stands, frankly returning his gaze. She stretches out a hand, which he takes.*)

You remember Antonia?

DECOUD: Of course. Last time we met your hair was in plaits.

ANTONIA: Welcome home.

(AVELLANOS *moves* DECOUD *along to* BARRIOS *and* GOULD.)

AVELLANOS: Gentlemen, this is my dear godson, Don Martin Decoud. General Barrios, Commandant of the garrison.

(BARRIOS *grasps* DECOUD*'s hand, and* DECOUD *does his best to suppress a fastidious shudder of disapproval.*)

And you remember Don Carlos, who has kindly financed this whole enterprise.

DECOUD: Yes, I believe we were at school together.

GOULD: Before I was sent back to England.

DECOUD: Well, gentlemen . . . (*He gestures upwards: above, a cradle is swinging out over the side of the ship and being lowered. Standing on the cradle, so glamorously striking that* DECOUD *breaks off in mid-sentence to look at him, is* NOSTROMO, *supervising the descent of a number of crates. As the camera moves in closer to the cradle, it becomes clear that the crates are all stamped with the silhouette of a lady of fashion and the legend:* MAISON WORTH.) (*Off-screen*) . . . I bring you from Paris the very latest fashions.

INT. UPSTAIRS IN THE CUSTOMS HOUSE. DAY

NOSTROMO *inserts a crowbar under the lid of one of the crates and prises it open. It springs back with a sound of splintering wood to reveal a layer of brand new rifles. He puts out a hand and runs it appreciatively over one of the weapons.*

He's in a strange, roomy corner office of the abandoned Customs House. Light filters in through closed shutters on two walls, one of which runs directly along the edge of the sea. In the corner is a long, official desk with quill pens and inkstands and a chair behind it. The room is so high, the roof-beams taper away into invisibility. The crate NOSTROMO *has opened is surrounded by a couple of dozen identical crates. He looks up at the sound of horses.*

EXT. CUSTOMS HOUSE. DAY

The GOULDS' *coach pulls up outside a bizarre unfinished building, eccentrically grandiose in conception, isolated on a promontory. The* GOULDS, AVELLANOS *and* ANTONIA *descend, while* GENERAL BARRIOS, *who has ridden up beside them, dismounts. They process towards the building, silhouetted against the sea.*

INT. CUSTOMS HOUSE. DAY

NOSTROMO *steps out on to the landing, as the group appears through one of the vast double doors and sets off up the stairs. They're in a most extraordinary building, an architect's folly like some huge derelict cathedral or Piranesi prison: the vast hall has an earth floor, disfigured in one corner by the fantastic shape of an anthill. The great staircase leads up to dark, deserted landings. There's no ceiling and heavy black beams disappear into the pitch of the roof.*

DECOUD: What is this place?

GOULD: It was supposed to be a new Customs House: but, as usual, they ran out of money before it could be completed.

INT. UPSTAIRS ROOM. DAY

BARRIOS *forges into the room and pulls out two of the rifles, handing one to* GOULD. *He examines it for a moment, his eye bright.*

BARRIOS: Montero has nothing like this. These are the only repeaters in Costaguana. Well done.

DECOUD: I don't know one end from the other. I took advice.

BARRIOS: Well, it was good advice.

AVELLANOS: Your arrival could hardly be more timely, my boy.

DECOUD: Oh?

GOULD: General Montero has just attempted a *coup*. It failed, through sheer luck it seems, but he escaped to his home province, where he's started to raise an army.

AVELLANOS: So these weapons may well be our salvation.

(DECOUD *is looking rather dubiously at* NOSTROMO.)

DECOUD: I take it their presence is to be kept secret.

GOULD: I'll vouch for Nostromo here: he's generally reckoned to be the most reliable man in Sulaco.

DECOUD: In that case, I'm delighted to meet you.

(*He extends a hand and* NOSTROMO *grasps it firmly, a sardonic glint in his eye.*)

INT. DINING-ROOM IN THE CASA GOULD. NIGHT

The dining-room is a large formal salon on the first floor, on the opposite side of the courtyard from the Gran Sala. GOULD *sits at the head of the table with* ANTONIA *on his right and* DECOUD *on his left.* MRS GOULD *is next to* DECOUD, *opposite* DON JOSÉ AVELLANOS.

AVELLANOS: I know your dear father would have been very proud of your decision to come back to your country in its hour of need.

MRS GOULD: So much in the country has improved, Señor Decoud: we can't risk slipping back into barbarism.

AVELLANOS: Martin knows that: we all read your magnificent piece in the *Parisian Review*.

DECOUD: It's just that in Paris, when they want an article about Costaguana, which, of course, is hardly ever, they don't know who else to ask. I wouldn't want you to have an exaggerated idea of my prowess as a journalist.

(GOULD *leans forward, speaks with his usual quiet authority.*)

GOULD: As I'm sure you know, one of the many things we lack in this country is an efficient and rational pro-Government newspaper. The gutter press has of course come out strongly in favour of Montero, who they stupidly suppose to be a man of the people. My partners in San Francisco understand this; and they've supplied me with plant and newsprint: now all we need is an experienced editor.

(*Silence. It takes a few seconds for* DECOUD *to understand what* GOULD *is proposing: then he's appalled. He shakes his head vigorously.*)

DECOUD: No, no, you don't understand: I came back out of curiosity. And I wanted to visit the United States, you know, see Yellowstone Park and Niagara Falls. I leave next month: I have my reservations.

(*They're all looking at him with various degrees of disapproval:*

none more so than ANTONIA, *who stares across the table at him, her expression openly contemptuous.* DECOUD, *almost panicking now, blurts out.*)
I've never really thought of myself as a serious journalist.

GOULD: Now's your chance.

ANTONIA: Have you ever thought of yourself as a serious anything?

MRS GOULD: The Government genuinely needs your help, Señor Decoud.

DECOUD: The Government? Or its business interests and foreign backers?

GOULD: Both.

(*Silence. Again* DECOUD *is miserably aware that all eyes are on him.*)

DECOUD: I'm sorry, it's out of the question.

EXT. CALLE DE LA CONSTITUCIÓN. NIGHT

DECOUD *emerges from the Casa Gould with* AVELLANOS *and* ANTONIA. *They cross the road and move towards the Casa Avellanos, which is more or less directly opposite.* AVELLANOS *moves very slowly; he looks old and tired.*

DECOUD: I think I'll take a stroll.

AVELLANOS: I need my rest, but Antonia will accompany you. It's wonderful to see you again, whatever you decide.

(ANTONIA *seems about to protest, but* AVELLANOS *kisses her on the forehead and disappears into his house, the door of which is already being held open by an ancient steward.*)

EXT. PLAZA MAYOR. NIGHT

DECOUD *and* ANTONIA *move slowly across the moonlit, practically deserted square in silence.*

DECOUD: You always used to get angry with me in Paris, do you remember?

ANTONIA: Did I?

DECOUD: Oh, yes, you were always very severe, like Charlotte Corday.

ANTONIA: Sometimes I didn't appreciate your cynicism.

DECOUD: I'm afraid for a journalist, cynicism is an occupational hazard.

ANTONIA: I thought you said you didn't think of yourself as a journalist.

DECOUD: All the same, it's what I am.

ANTONIA: Then let me appeal to you, as a friend . . .

DECOUD: I'm not sure I believe men and women can be friends.

(*They've come to a halt now, in the centre of the square, and* DECOUD *is aware that he has her total attention.*)

Look, as far as I know, Ribiera is a decent enough man; but I can't run a propaganda sheet in support of a dictatorship, can I? In Paris I have a reputation as a liberal.

ANTONIA: In Paris all they care about is theory. Where do you suppose Montero picked up all his high-flown ideals? It doesn't make him any less of a stupid thug. Didn't you meet him over there?

DECOUD: I know he used to be at the Legation, serving at table: all I remember is his thumb in my soup.

ANTONIA: My father is a genuine idealist and patriot: for which Guzman Bento tortured him half to death and let my mother die in fear and despair. How can we allow all that to happen again?

DECOUD: I can't help feeling there's been a failure of the imagination. Why wasn't Montero bribed, like everyone else? Shouldn't he have been offered his weight in gold and packed off back to Europe?

ANTONIA: He wants more than that. He wants everything.

(DECOUD *shakes his head and starts walking again, sighing in exasperation.*)

DECOUD: Why don't you come with me when I leave? Abandon this preposterous country?

ANTONIA: You should be ashamed of yourself, Martin. This is my country. And it's yours as well.

(*She's spoken gently to him, and for once* DECOUD *is at a loss for words. After a pause, she speaks again.*)

Tell me, what was your real reason for coming home?

(DECOUD *hesitates, nerving himself to give an honest answer.*)

DECOUD: If I said it was to see you, I expect you'd disapprove of me even more.

(ANTONIA *hesitates in her turn.*)

ANTONIA: Not necessarily.

(They've arrived in the corner of the Plaza, at the end of the colonnades, looking up at a first-floor window. ANTONIA *points up at it and* DECOUD, *not at the moment understanding, looks up himself.)*

DISSOLVE

EXT. PLAZA MAYOR. DAY

The window now contains the large black letters of the word 'PORVENIR'. *Below, in the Plaza,* DECOUD *and* ANTONIA *stand looking up at the window,* ANTONIA *flushed with excitement, her eyes sparkling and* DECOUD*'s usual wary expression tinged with a certain exhilaration.*

A caption:

SIX MONTHS LATER

INT. PRINTING-ROOM. DAY

The new presses in their first-floor back room roar into action. DECOUD *waits to collect the first copy of his eight-page broadsheet. Under the banner heading* Porvenir, *the bold headlines scream out:*

CIVIL WAR RAGES

Montero massacres civilians

INT. EDITOR'S OFFICE. NIGHT

DECOUD*'s office is on the second and top floor, with a dramatic view down across the whole of the Plaza Mayor. He turns away from the window, settles down in his new chair at his new desk, takes a fresh sheet of paper and begins to write.*

MONTAGE OF PRINTING PRESS AND HEADLINES

'BUTCHER' MONTERO MARCHES NORTH

CIVIL WAR ENTERS SIXTH MONTH

CAYTA UNDER SIEGE FROM MONTERO'S ARMY

A front page is entirely given over to a ferocious caricature of MONTERO *eating a baby under the simple banner headline:* ATROCITY.

The presses continue to roll.

INT. BILLIARD ROOM OF THE AMARILLA CLUB. DAY

GENERAL BARRIOS *is on his feet, with a glass in his hand, in the smoke-filled billiard room of the aristocrats' club in Sulaco. Dressed in his usual tattered uniform, he's addressing a company which consists of* DECOUD, AVELLANOS, GOULD, *and a new face, a young officer,* COLONEL SOTILLO, *handsome in a shifty kind of way, soft-spoken but self-confident, his uniform impeccable; and something weak and vicious in his face.*

BARRIOS: All right: now. (*He puts down his glass and, to everyone's surprise, unbuckles his leather belt and slams it down on the billiard table.*) Here's the coastline. (*He twists the belt into a shape roughly analogous to the north-west coast of South America; then he reaches for the two white billiard balls, placing them up against his belt.*) This is us in Sulaco; and this is the port of Cayta. (*South of the left-hand ball and well inland, he places the red ball.*) And here's the capital. (*Out of his sleeve he produces an alarmingly stained yellowish handkerchief, which he drops north of the capital, close to the port of Cayta.*) Montero's army is here, besieging Cayta. I propose to take ship from here to Cayta, with my men and your rifles, engage him and . . . (*He picks up the handkerchief and blows his nose sonorously; then he drops the handkerchief back into its former position.*) Couldn't be simpler.

DECOUD: One question.

BARRIOS: Yes?

DECOUD: Won't that leave us completely undefended?

(BARRIOS *sighs. He puts his glass down and with some difficulty wrestles off one of his red boots, which he then bangs down on the table between the billiard ball which represents Sulaco and the others.*)

BARRIOS: Now what do you suppose that is?

DECOUD: The mountains.

BARRIOS: No army has ever been able to march across those mountains in winter. So what chance has that bald imposter? On the other hand, if he succeeds in taking Cayta . . . (*He picks up the handkerchief again and drops it so that it covers the billiard ball representing Cayta.*) . . . he will have access to shipping and he will be able to sail around and attack us by sea. So we must stop him in his tracks.

(*At this point,* GOULD *intervenes.*)

GOULD: What plans do we have to protect the cable office at Esmeralda? I don't want to lose contact with San Francisco.

BARRIOS: Esmeralda. (*He picks up the cube of blue chalk and places it a little way up the 'coast', east of Sulaco, so that Sulaco falls between it and the 'mountains'. Then he thoughtfully refills his glass with some poisonous-looking colourless liquid from an unlabelled bottle and takes a long draught.*) Perhaps we should send some reinforcements. Especially as I happen to know the officer in charge of the garrison is a hopeless alcoholic.

(*He drains his glass. Meanwhile,* SOTILLO *leans forward, his eyes bright.*)

SOTILLO: I would be honoured to take Esmeralda in hand, General.

(BARRIOS *grunts sceptically.*)

BARRIOS: That'd get you out of the front line, wouldn't it?

SOTILLO: Of course, if you think . . .

AVELLANOS: If you could spare him, General, I'm sure Colonel Sotillo is an ideal candidate for Military Governor.

BARRIOS *turns his glittering eye on* SOTILLO *for a moment.*

BARRIOS: Oh, very well; let the ladies of Esmeralda have their chance, eh? (*He snorts with laughter, then turns to face them all.*) So, gentlemen, if you agree, I can promise you this: in three weeks I shall bring you back that insolent Montero. In a cage! (*And so saying, he grabs the red ball and rolls it diagonally across the billiard table, fast and accurate into the corner pocket.*

DECOUD *jots something down on his notepad, shaking his head in some incredulity.*)

EXT. SIDE-STREET. NIGHT

DECOUD *makes his way cautiously down the dark and dusty alley. He's approaching a one-storey adobe* posada *or inn, from which the sound of a Mexican-style orchestra bursts, while yellow light streams through the open doorway, into which* DECOUD *disappears.*

INT. POSADA. NIGHT

NOSTROMO *sits at a plain table, a Havana cigar between his lips,* PAQUITA *on his arm, a bottle of tequila open in front of him. He looks up, surprised, as* DECOUD*'s shadow falls across the table. Then he pushes a chair out with his foot, motions* DECOUD *to sit down and summons a glass from a passing bar attendant.*

DECOUD: I was told I might find you here.

NOSTROMO: How can I help you, Signor?

DECOUD: I was also told that is always your first question.

(NOSTROMO *is pouring a drink out for* DECOUD*; he's not at all put out by* DECOUD*'s remark.*)

NOSTROMO: I find it saves time.

(DECOUD *smiles, takes a sip of tequila, grimaces.*)

DECOUD: It's a journalist's job to get to know remarkable men. And I hear you know everything that goes on in the town.

NOSTROMO: It's true.

DECOUD: Then do you mind if I ask you one or two questions?

NOSTROMO: I must tell you, Signor, I never read your paper.

DECOUD: Very wise.

NOSTROMO: Let me guess what it is you want to know.

(*He drains his tequila, pours another and fills* DECOUD*'s glass.*)

Now the army has sailed away with those guns you didn't want me to see, you're wondering if the police will be able to keep control of the town.

DECOUD: I hear rumours that there's likely to be rioting.

NOSTROMO: Almost certainly, I would say. So, I spoke to my dockers last night; and they agreed that when it happens, they will take to the streets and help restore order.

(DECOUD *has found this an increasingly surprising conversation. Now he frowns for a moment, considering this last proposition, before deciding to change tack.*)

DECOUD: Tell me, why did you decide to settle in Costaguana?

NOSTROMO: To make my fortune.

DECOUD: And why should the dockers decide to come out on the side of the authorities?

NOSTROMO: We Europeans should stick together, don't you agree?

DECOUD: I do, even though I'm not a European. The question I keep asking myself is what on earth ever prompted me to come back to this godforsaken country . . .

(NOSTROMO *contemplates him shrewdly for a moment.*)

NOSTROMO: A woman?

(DECOUD *is once again taken aback by* NOSTROMO*'s perceptiveness.*)

INT. GRAN SALA IN THE CASA GOULD. NIGHT

This is now a room of dazzling opulence: the mirrors and chandeliers sparkle, the French windows to the balcony are open and hung with damask curtains, a small orchestra sits on a dais at one end of the room, heroically attempting a waltz, and one of the two large rugs has been turned back to make a red-tiled dance floor. There's an atmosphere of forced and hectic gaiety: and ANTONIA *dances by in* DECOUD*'s arms.*

DECOUD: Of course from over there in Paris, our whole country seems like some exaggerated joke. But when you're here, watching the entire garrison embark under the command of some boastful, one-eyed alcoholic, it's somehow no longer amusing.

ANTONIA: The purpose of history, Martin, is not to provide you with a source of entertainment.

DECOUD: No, our history is to tear at one another's throats with such imbecilic ferocity, we fail to notice the foreign speculators quietly helping themselves to our resources.

ANTONIA: Now you sound like Montero himself.

(*As they pass the large double doors, the camera stops to observe, as* DECOUD *and* ANTONIA *waltz out of frame, the arrival of* DR MONYGHAM. *While all the other guests are in full evening dress,* MONYGHAM*'s sole concession to the occasion is a short cream linen jacket worn over his check shirt. He stands in the doorway, looking around disconsolately, very well aware of the hostile or curious glances of the other guests. He makes a decision, turns on his heel and is about to leave, when* MRS GOULD, *who has broken away from a nearby group, materializes at his elbow.*)

MRS GOULD: Doctor, how very good of you to come.

MONYGHAM: I was . . .

MRS GOULD: Won't you come and talk to me for a while? I've been danced off my feet.

(*She takes his arm and begins leading him across the room, watched by several of the guests.*)

MONYGHAM: You would hardly guess the country is in the grip of civil war.

MRS GOULD: We thought it important to keep up morale.

MONYGHAM: Most people prefer not to think at all.

(*The waltz comes to an end, couples stand and applaud, and the camera stays on* DECOUD *and* ANTONIA, *as* MRS GOULD *and* MONYGHAM *move past them.* DECOUD *takes* ANTONIA*'s arm.*)

DECOUD: Let's get some air.

(*As the orchestra strikes up again with a lively polka,* DECOUD *steers* ANTONIA *through the central French windows out on to the balcony, talking in an undertone as he goes.*)

Why is that sinister doctor so unpopular?

ANTONIA: I don't know: there's some mystery in his past.

DECOUD: But Señora Gould likes him.

ANTONIA: She of course is a saint.

DECOUD: It's said she thinks of nothing but her schools and her hospitals and her orphans and every sick old man in the province.

ANTONIA: And her husband.

(*A tall hawk-faced priest walks past in front of them (by now they are on the balcony, looking back into the room) and the camera follows him across to* MRS GOULD, *to whom he bows politely.*)

MRS GOULD: Good evening, father.

(*As the priest moves off,* MRS GOULD *is instantly aware of* MONYGHAM*'s discomfort and distaste.*)

What's the matter?

MONYGHAM: Priests. They make me nervous. That was one of the things I liked most about being in the jungle. No priests.

MRS GOULD: You were happy in the jungle?

MONYGHAM: No. But it healed me. And I would rather spend my time with the most primitive tribe than mix with the cream of Sulaco society. Present company excepted.

(MRS GOULD *smiles gracefully at his clumsy compliment. Then she frowns slightly, her attention caught by a small, depressed-*

looking man with a drooping moustache and ill-fitting clothes: his name is HIRSCH. *He shuffles by and the camera follows him as he approaches* GOULD, *who is dancing the polka with one of his guests.* HIRSCH *raises a hand and opens his mouth to speak; but* GOULD *glides smoothly past, ignoring him completely. The camera moves with* GOULD *and his partner, until they pass the open window where it stops to observe* DECOUD *and* ANTONIA *on the balcony, watched by a censorious group of seated, elderly women, who are obviously scandalized by the extreme impropriety of the tête-à-tête.* DECOUD, *suddenly aware of their disapproval, pointedly turns his back on the room.*)

EXT. BALCONY AND CALLE DE LA CONSTITUCIÓN. NIGHT

DECOUD*'s* POV*: moving up the street, his cigar glowing in the darkness, is the powerful and enigmatic figure of* NOSTROMO, *enveloped in his poncho. He passes through the pool of light cast by a street lamp.*

DECOUD: Look: the illustrious Nostromo. Probably the most important man in Sulaco. Apart from Señor Gould.

ANTONIA: You think so?

DECOUD: I envy him.

ANTONIA: Why?

DECOUD: Men are afraid of him and women adore him. You hear nothing else except how strong and courageous and incorruptible he is. He's a hero. Why wouldn't I envy him?

ANTONIA: And are those your highest aspirations?

(DECOUD *looks at her for a moment.*)

DECOUD: No, Antonia: you are my highest aspiration.

(*Before* ANTONIA *can answer, she's interrupted by some sort of disturbance inside the gran sala; they both turn to look back into the room.*)

INT. GRAN SALA. NIGHT

What's happening in the room is that DON JOSÉ AVELLANOS *is standing on the dais, tapping a glass with a spoon, until he's rewarded with silence.*

AVELLANOS: I want you all to join me in a toast to our President: now that reinforcements are at hand, he will not fail us. To Don Vincente Ribiera!

(He raises his glass and all the guests join him in an enthusiastic toast.)

INT. COURTYARD OF THE PRESIDENTIAL PALACE IN SANTA MARTA. DAWN

Against a whitewashed wall stands the dishevelled figure of DON VINCENTE RIBIERA *himself, his frock-coat torn and dusty. He's quaking and tears are rolling down his plump cheeks. Suddenly, there's a volley of gunfire and* RIBIERA *slides to the ground.*

ANOTHER ANGLE *reveals the firing squad; and the fact that all this has taken place under the gimlet-eyed supervision of* GENERAL MONTERO*; who now turns away, grimly satisfied.*

INT./EXT. BALCONY AND GRAN SALA. NIGHT

The party is still in full swing; and DECOUD *and* ANTONIA *are still on the balcony, locked in passionate debate.*

DECOUD: Separation.

ANTONIA: Separation?

DECOUD: Secession.

ANTONIA: No, no, no.

DECOUD: Listen, Don Carlos's mine is very probably the greatest *fact* in the whole of South America. And the rest of Costaguana has always hung round our necks like a millstone. So why shouldn't we form a new, small, prosperous state? The Republic of Sulaco?

ANTONIA: I don't know what to make of you, Martin; first you make fun of everything about our country: then you suddenly reveal yourself as a patriot.

DECOUD: I'm not a patriot, I'm a lover. I've failed to separate you from your country; now, the only thing I can think of is to separate your country from its infinitely squalid government. This will be the subject of my next leader.

(He's aware now of the phalanx of elderly citizens staring at him and ANTONIA *in mute disapproval. With a truculent expression, he leans forward, and unhooks the curtain, so that it falls across, concealing them.* ANTONIA *makes a protesting move but* DECOUD *intercepts her hand.)*

ANTONIA: But people will talk.

DECOUD: They will anyway. And my time is running out.

ANTONIA: I don't know what you mean.

DECOUD: Three times a week I write an editorial systematically insulting Montero. It's been fatal to my self-respect; and very shortly it will be fatal to me.

ANTONIA: Are you assuming Montero will win?

DECOUD: Of course he'll win. He's brutal and stupid enough, how can he fail? Everyone knows he carries a death-list with him; and one of the first names on it is mine. I shall go to the wall.

(ANTONIA *looks up at him suddenly, her eyes filling with tears.*)

ANTONIA: Oh, Martin, you'll make me cry.

(DECOUD*'s expression softens; he's moved by her concern. Impulsively, he puts his arms around her.*)

INT. GRAN SALA. NIGHT

The observers in the room are scandalized to see the two silhouettes of DECOUD *and* ANTONIA *merge behind the curtain in a passionate embrace.*

DISSOLVE

EXT. VERANDAH OF THE CASA GOULD. NIGHT

GOULD *stands at the top of the staircase saying goodnight to his guests. Last in line, a determined glint in his eyes, is* HIRSCH. *He speaks with a heavy German accent.*

HIRSCH: My name is Hirsch, Don Carlos. This is a very great honour.

GOULD: Delighted.

HIRSCH: Ah, these civil wars, Don Carlos. What a foolishness!

GOULD: Quite.

(*He smiles thinly and releases* HIRSCH*'s hand: but* HIRSCH *only edges nearer, adopting a confidential tone.*)

HIRSCH: May I say a word?

GOULD: Well . . .

HIRSCH: Dynamite.

GOULD: I beg your pardon?

HIRSCH: I happen to have some friends in Hamburg who specialize in dynamite. As a mine-owner, I thought . . .

GOULD: As a mine-owner, I already have thought, Señor

Hirsch. I have enough dynamite to bring down the whole San Tomé mountain.

HIRSCH: Ah.

GOULD: And if necessary, I shall have no hesitation in using it.

HIRSCH: Of course.

GOULD: So thank you and goodnight.

(HIRSCH *inclines his head and sets off down the stairs, shoulders bowed.* GOULD *watches him go, pensive, already thinking of other things.*)

EXT. PLAZA MAYOR. NIGHT

DECOUD, *walking briskly, turns left into the deserted Plaza. He's on his way towards the* Porvenir *offices, when he's intercepted by a small man in his shirt-sleeves, running at full pelt across the Plaza, obviously greatly agitated.*

EXT. VERANDAH OF THE CASA GOULD. NIGHT

GOULD *sits, deep in thought, sipping a cognac, a lone figure surrounded by deep shadows. He looks up to see* DECOUD *hurrying up the stone staircase, with* BASILIO *puffing along behind him. Almost at the top of the stairs,* DECOUD *turns to* BASILIO.

DECOUD: Ah, Basilio: Señorita Antonia has left her fan somewhere.

BASILIO: I haven't seen it, Don Martin.

DECOUD: Try looking down on the patio.

(BASILIO *frowns, puzzled, but sets off down the stairs;* GOULD *is also watching this in some perplexity. Now* DECOUD *comes over to him and begins whispering in an urgent undertone.*)

Bernhardt from the Cable Company stopped me on the Plaza with some serious news.

GOULD: What?

DECOUD: It seems Montero turned back from Cayta and marched on the capital. There was a pitched battle with Ribiera's forces, which he won. Then he invaded the capital. The President-Dictator has been executed without trial. The final telegram in this sequence is addressed directly from Montero to you.

(*He hands* GOULD *a cable, over which the latter swiftly runs his eye.*)

We should never have let Barrios leave Sulaco.

(GOULD *looks up from the telegram and springs to his feet.*)

GOULD: Thank you. And now please excuse me.

DECOUD: Of course.

(*He extracts* ANTONIA*'s fan from his sleeve.*)

EXT. PATIO. NIGHT

DECOUD *comes clattering down the steps from the verandah.* BASILIO*'s searching in some corner with an oil-lamp; now he looks up to see* DECOUD *flourishing the fan.*

DECOUD: Thank you, Basilio, I've found it.

(BASILIO*'s just taking this aboard, when* GOULD *leans over the banister and barks a crisp order.*)

GOULD: Saddle my horse.

INT. MRS GOULD'S BEDROOM. NIGHT

MRS GOULD *is sitting up in the four-poster bed, wearing her dressing-gown, reading. She looks up, surprised, as* GOULD *strides into the room, boots and spurs in his hand.*

MRS GOULD: What is it?

GOULD: Montero has won. He requires a donation.

(*He's begun pulling on his boots, seated with his back to her on the bed.*)

MRS GOULD: What sort of a donation?

GOULD: Six months' supply of silver. Down to the last bar.

(*His boots are on; he rises and moves straight to the door, his spurs clinking.* MRS GOULD *scrambles out of bed to follow him.*)

INT. CORRIDOR. NIGHT

MRS GOULD *hurries after* GOULD, *oddly illuminated by the oil-lamp he's carrying.*

MRS GOULD: What will you do?

GOULD: I still don't think he'll be able to bring his army over the mountains. But let's assume he manages it. It still gives us time to bring the silver down and get it out of the country.

(MRS GOULD *looks apprehensive.*)

MRS GOULD: But is that wise?

GOULD: It's essential.

EXT. VERANDAH. NIGHT

GOULD *sets down his lamp and strides across the verandah. Below, his horse is already saddled and held by the groom. At the top of the staircase, however,* MRS GOULD *puts a hand on his arm and stops him.*

MRS GOULD: Won't you talk to me about it?

GOULD: I thought you understood. I thought we had said all there was to say a long time ago. There's no turning back now. We can only go forward.

(*His tone is so coldly determined that* MRS GOULD*'s hand has dropped away from him.*)

MRS GOULD: How far?

GOULD: Any distance.

MRS GOULD: But always to success?

(GOULD *looks down at her, his expression icily unyielding.*)

GOULD: There is no alternative.

(*He bends to kiss her hands, then turns and clatters down the stairs.*)

EXT. PATIO. NIGHT

GOULD *swings into the saddle and takes the reins; the groom falls back.* MRS GOULD, *seized by a sudden access of fear, calls down to him.*

MRS GOULD: Charley.

(*He looks up at her, a trace of impatience in his expression.*)

Perhaps we should have left it alone.

GOULD: No. Impossible.

(*He spurs on his horse and canters out of the patio.*)

EXT. CALLE DE LA CONSTITUCIÓN. NIGHT

As GOULD *emerges from the house, he encounters* NOSTROMO, *returning from the Plaza Mayor on his silver-grey mare. He raises a hand to* GOULD.

NOSTROMO: Signor.

(*Something about his solid, confidence-inspiring presence prompts* GOULD *to lean towards him and speak in an undertone.*)

GOULD: You should know. There's been a *coup* in the capital. The President is dead. As soon as the news comes through, I've no doubt there'll be chaos in the town. You may want to make your dispositions.

NOSTROMO: Where are you riding, Signor?

GOULD: To the mine. I need to get my silver out of the country before any of these gangsters are in a position to steal it.

NOSTROMO: You need some help?

(GOULD *considers his calm and authoritative demeanour for a moment.*)

GOULD: Yes. Yes, I'd be most grateful.

NOSTROMO: *Andiamo.*

(*He wheels his horse and the two of them set off, galloping towards the Plaza.*)

INT. MRS GOULD'S BEDROOM. NIGHT

MRS GOULD *comes back into the room, thoughtful and upset. As she crosses to the window, her eye falls on: the silver ingot on her bureau. She lets her fingers drift across its surface, as she moves to look out of the window. At the same time, a strange, jolting, clattering sound begins.*

INT. SILVER WAGON. NIGHT

An image, which is not immediately intelligible, like an unstable quicksilver staircase: it's a pile of silver ingots, loaded loose into a wagon, shifting and sliding, as the mules gallop down towards Sulaco.

EXT. LOWER WORKINGS OF THE MINE. NIGHT

OVERHEAD SHOT: *the wagon is one of half a dozen now crashing down the track which leads away from the mine village and through the great San Tomé gates.* GOULD *is at the head of the column, which consists of a couple of dozen armed guards in green and white company ponchos, all carrying Winchesters; and* NOSTROMO *is bringing up the rear.*

EXT. HOSPITAL AT THE MINE. NIGHT

A REVERSE SHOT *shows* DR MONYGHAM, *watching the exodus, out on the balcony of his hospital, in his white housecoat. For once, his sardonic expression has given way to a look of genuine concern.*

EXT. COASTAL PLAIN. NIGHT

The column crashes through the cactus jungle.

EXT. GATES OF SULACO. NIGHT

The old city gates, seen from within, the mountains towering above, black shapes in the darkness. GOULD *gallops through the opening in the crumbling walls, followed by the wagon train.* NOSTROMO, *at the rear, pulls down the bandanna he has wrapped over his mouth and nose against the dust of the plain.*

INT. DECOUD'S OFFICE. NIGHT

DECOUD *looks up from his writing at the sound of the approaching wagon train. He lays down his pen, gets up and hurries to the window.*

EXT. PLAZA MAYOR. NIGHT

DECOUD*'s* POV*: the wagon train careers across the Plaza, its clatter reverberating around the deserted square.*

INT. GRAN SALA. NIGHT

MRS GOULD, *in her dressing-gown, hurries across the huge room and opens the central French window.*

EXT. CALLE DE LA CONSTITUCIÓN. NIGHT

GOULD *leads the wagon train down the street, his face set in grim concentration.*

EXT. BALCONY OF THE CASA GOULD. NIGHT

MRS GOULD *emerges on to the balcony and waves to her husband.*

EXT. CALLE DE LA CONSTITUCIÓN. NIGHT

GOULD *gallops by under the balcony. He doesn't look up.*

EXT. BALCONY. NIGHT

MRS GOULD *watches him, shaken and upset, as the wagon train thunders by.*

EXT. NEAR THE ALBERGO D'ITALIA UNA. NIGHT

A wagon wheel strikes sparks off the railway line, as the column crashes across the tracks.

EXT. ALBERGO. NIGHT

As the wagon train hurtles past the inn, TERESA VIOLA, *in her dressing-gown, stumbles out of the ground floor room where she has taken to sleeping, her face taut with pain.*

NOSTROMO *sees her, reins in his horse and jumps down. Dialogue in Italian.*

TERESA: What are you doing?

NOSTROMO: There may be rioting in the town today; they need to get the silver away.

TERESA: What does it matter to you?

NOSTROMO: I promised I would help.

TERESA: Your place is here with us, if there's going to be trouble.

NOSTROMO: I'll come back when I can.

(*He jumps up on his horse again.* TERESA *grabs at his sleeve.*)

TERESA: Don't leave us alone!

NOSTROMO: Goodbye.

TERESA: Think of the children!

(*For a second,* NOSTROMO *hesitates, struck by her intensity; then he gallops away into the darkness.*)

EXT. ENTRADA PASS. NIGHT

A snow-framed wooden sign reads: ENTRADA PASS: *6,748 metres.*

A blizzard is blowing. The awesome figure of GENERAL MONTERO, *fur-coated, his feet wrapped in bloodstained rags, upright in the saddle. On his emaciated horse, he struggles upwards across the rocky plateau, into the driving snow, his ragged army, mostly on foot, straggling behind him in irregular files.*

EXT. PLAZA MAYOR. DAWN

The Plaza is deserted and in muted light, the sun having not yet risen above the mountain range. A dust devil drifts lazily across the square.

INT. DECOUD'S OFFICE. DAWN

The scratch of a pen. DECOUD *is still at his desk, writing. A faint breeze rattles the jalousies and stirs the papers on his desk.* DECOUD *looks up, thoughtful, frowning at some premonition. He gets up and steps over to the window, pushing aside the blind to look down across the Plaza.*

EXT. PLAZA MAYOR. DAWN

DECOUD*'s* POV*: A menacingly silent mob is moving across the gardens of the Alameda towards the Intendencia, which is guarded by a squad of armed policemen. The mob comes to a halt, facing the inadequately defended building; most of the attackers are primitively armed with clubs or machetes, even the occasional elderly rifle. Even at this distance, there's a whiff of genuine danger.*

INT. DECOUD'S OFFICE. DAWN

DECOUD *steps away from the window, opens a drawer and takes out a small, pearl-handled revolver and some ammunition, slipping them into a side-pocket. Then he begins moving towards the door.*

EXT. PLAZA MAYOR. DAWN

DECOUD *emerges from the* Porvenir *office and advances cautiously behind the colonnades, looking out across the square. A few yards along, he recognizes a tethered silver-grey mare. Turning in the other direction he sees, through the window of a barber-shop, a solitary customer receiving a shave from a lone barber. He steps through the glass door.*

INT. BARBER-SHOP. DAWN

The BARBER *looks up, his demeanour jittery, as* DECOUD *appears.*

BARBER: We are closed, señor.

DECOUD: No, no; I wanted to speak to your customer.

(*The customer, with the last specks of shaving-foam still adhering to his chin, is* NOSTROMO. *He looks up, relaxed, as* DECOUD *approaches and the* BARBER *cleans off the remaining foam with a hot towel.*)

Any minute now, I'd say they were going to begin attacking the Intendencia.

NOSTROMO: There's no one in there. Most of them have gone down to the harbour.

BARBER: May we go now, señor? Please.

NOSTROMO: Show me.

(*The* BARBER *grabs up a mirror and holds it up behind* NOSTROMO, *so that he can study the back of his head. This he does, with some care, before finally grunting in acknowledgement that the task has been satisfactorily completed. He gets to his feet, brushes himself off and strolls over to the entrance with* DECOUD, *pulling on his jacket.*)

EXT. COLONNADES. DAWN

NOSTROMO *and* DECOUD *pause, as behind them, the* BARBER *hastily bolts and shutters his shop.*

EXT. PLAZA MAYOR. DAWN

Their POV*: in the opposite corner of the Plaza, the mob advances. Stones start to fly; the tinkle of broken glass.*

DECOUD *looks the other way: next to the Amarilla Club a barricade has been built across the entrance to the Calle de la Constitución.*

DECOUD: I'm going to the club.

NOSTROMO: Very wise, señor. Your newspaper is not much loved. (*He points across the Plaza at the mob.*) They know Montero is on his way. Their aim will be to steal as much as they can before he arrives. But my men are waiting; we'll look after our own.

DECOUD: Good luck.

(*He sets off across the corner of the Plaza in the direction of the Club, as* NOSTROMO *mounts his mare.*)

INT. BILLIARD ROOM OF THE AMARILLA CLUB. DAWN

The first-floor room has been transformed. The French windows are open and the billiard table has been up-ended to form a barricade, behind which a line of members stand, including DECOUD,*who has been issued with a large and unwieldy sporting gun. Dust swirls in through the open window. A Club servant, still in his livery, has been trussed up in the velvet cords, which usually hold back the heavy curtains, and stuck in a corner. An ominous silence.*

EXT. SIDE-STREET OFF THE PLAZA MAYOR. DAWN

NOSTROMO *is mounted, at the head of a column of silent dockers, many of whom are armed with primitive rifles, waiting. From their position, they can see that the mob's attack has now begun in earnest. They begin to surge forward, but* NOSTROMO *raises a hand, judging that the time to make a move has not yet arrived.*

INT. AMARILLA CLUB. DAY

DECOUD *watches, his face close against the window.*

EXT. AMARILLA CLUB. DAY

His POV*: the mob finally overcomes the inadequate police defence and surges into the Intendencia. The wind has risen and dust is beginning to swirl across the Plaza.*

INT. STAIRCASE AND GAMACHO'S OFFICE IN THE INTENDENCIA. DAY

The mob rampages up the stairs and into the great room, where they immediately set about smashing the mirrors, setting fire to the curtains, slashing the paintings and swinging from the chandelier.

EXT. PLAZA MAYOR. DAY

TRACKING SHOT; *clouds of dust billow across the square, concealing the group of rioters, who move purposefully to and fro. A pile of gilt and plush furniture blazes outside the Intendencia in a merry bonfire. Scattered corpses of policemen lie at undignified angles; the survivors have regrouped behind the barricades.*

The camera comes to rest outside the offices of the Porvenir: *and a few seconds later, a printing press comes hurtling through the plate-glass window which bears the newspaper's name and crashes into the square below, spilling type in all directions.*

INT./EXT. AMARILLA CLUB. DAY

DECOUD *watches ruefully, as another printing press crashes into the square.*

DECOUD: I see my critics are out in force.

(*Several rioters start picking up pieces of metal debris and hurling them at the Club. A large steel nut whistles past* DECOUD *and shatters a full-length mirror on the far wall. And suddenly, below, an armed group materializes from the dust and starts firing up at the Club. The Club members return the fire and* DECOUD *tucks his rifle into his shoulder and squeezes the trigger. The gun goes off with a thunderous roar;* DECOUD *groans, bruised by the recoil, and begins massaging his shoulder.*)

EXT. PLAZA MAYOR. DAY

Among the purposeful, shadowy rioters flitting through the dust is a darting, terrified figure, erratic as a headless chicken: it's a panic-stricken HIRSCH.

He ducks into the colonnade, where he's immediately transfixed by the shattered frontage of Anzani's emporium, the principal general store in the town. Looters are pouring out of the shop wearing fur stoles, carrying whole hams, flourishing bottles, staggering under the weight of fish tanks or monumental urns. Following some entirely illogical impulse, HIRSCH *ducks into the store.*

INT. ANZANI'S EMPORIUM. DAY

The shop is bedlam, as many items smashed as stolen, full of struggling looters. But almost immediately, HIRSCH *stumbles over something that makes his eyes goggle in horror. It's the body of* ANZANI, *a middle-aged Syrian of dignified proportions, who's lying on his back, an expression of the purest astonishment on his face, one hand closed around the hilt of a knife protruding from his stomach.*

HIRSCH, *completely out of control, plunges on through the shop and out the back entrance.*

EXT. ANZANI'S BACK YARD. DAY

HIRSCH *erupts out of Anzani's, dashes across the yard and is propelled, purely by fear, up a six-foot wall. He scrambles over the top of the wall, losing one of his shoes in the process, and vanishes.*

EXT. BALCONY OF THE CASA GOULD. DAY

MRS GOULD *hears the swelling sound of the approaching mob, the crackle of gunfire from the defenders behind the barricade on the Calle de la Constitución, as smoke and dust swirl down the street. She withdraws, looking a little shaken.*

INT. GRAN SALA OF THE CASA GOULD. DAY

MRS GOULD *steps back into the room, closing the French doors behind her. She still looks worried, but, seeing at once that* BASILIO *is white with terror, she reverts to her customary confidence-inspiring calm.*

INT./EXT. AMARILLA CLUB. DAY

DECOUD *fires another round, part of a volley from the club members. His* POV: *down below, the mob is storming the barricade.*

EXT. PLAZA MAYOR. DAY

Behind the barricade the police defenders come to a spontaneous decision, turn and run away down the Calle de la Constitución. It takes a moment for this to sink in; then the mob rushes forward, scrambling over the barricade.

INT./EXT. GRAN SALA OF THE CASA GOULD. DAY

MRS GOULD *shrinks back from the window, concealing herself: but below, on the street, the mob streams by, intent on some other purpose than attacking the mansions of the rich.*

EXT. SIDE-STREET OFF THE PLAZA MAYOR. DAY

NOSTROMO *judges the moment has come: he raises his silver whistle to his lips, gives a blast, raises a hand and spurs his mare forward.*

NOSTROMO: *Avanti!*

(*The dockers surge forward in his wake.*)

INT./EXT. AMARILLA CLUB. DAY

DECOUD *watches, as, below,* NOSTROMO *gallops across the square towards the barricade and urges his mare to vault over it.*

EXT. BALCONY OF THE CASA GOULD. DAY

Cautiously, MRS GOULD *emerges, in time to see:*

EXT. CALLE DE LA CONSTITUCIÓN. DAY

NOSTROMO, *plunging down the street, his followers, the dockers, on foot, in hot pursuit.*

EXT. PLAZA MAYOR. DAY

Clattering past the cathedral into the square, driving a plain wagon taken from the mine workings, is DR MONYGHAM. *He's driving much too fast and the wagon tilts perilously as it turns into the Plaza. He steadies the vehicle and drives over to the barricade, where he's obliged to come to a halt and jumps down. Then he begins, as best he can, to scramble over the man-made barrier.*

EXT. BALCONY. DAY

Clouds of dust drift down the Calle de la Constitución, when suddenly MRS GOULD*'s attention is caught by something.*

EXT. CALLE DE LA CONSTITUCIÓN. DAY

DR MONYGHAM *climbs down the barricade facing inwards, so it's not until he reaches the ground and turns, that he becomes aware of three or four menacing stragglers from the mob, who are standing waiting for this obviously rich European to make his landing. They begin to close in on* MONYGHAM, *when they're stopped in their tracks by a clear and unexpected* VOICE:

MRS GOULD: (*Off-screen*) Doctor.

(*One of the stragglers turns and we take his* POV*:* MRS GOULD *stands a little way off. She's holding, quite casually, but unmistakeably, a revolver.* MONYGHAM *hurries to join her as the stragglers melt away.*)

EXT. ENTRANCE TO THE CASA GOULD. DAY

With extreme caution, BASILIO *opens the small door set into the gate a crack to admit* MONYGHAM *and* MRS GOULD.

EXT. PATIO IN THE CASA GOULD. DAY

MONYGHAM *follows* MRS GOULD *into the dust-laden patio. He looks sheepish and disoriented and his clothes are grey with dust.*

MONYGHAM: Well, thank you.

MRS GOULD: This is not a day for paying calls, Doctor.

MONYGHAM: I wanted to make sure you, I mean, the house was safe.

MRS GOULD: As you see.

MONYGHAM: I thought your husband might have some instructions for me.

MRS GOULD: He's not here.

(*She's said this as casually as she can manage, but* MONYGHAM *is unable to conceal his sense of shock.*)

MONYGHAM: Not here?

MRS GOULD: I imagine he's still dealing with the silver.

MONYGHAM: So are you on your own?

MRS GOULD: No, the servants are . . .

(*She breaks off.* MONYGHAM *has looked away, conscious of*

revealing too much. The uproar from the Plaza fills the silence.) I'm glad you're here, Doctor. I'm afraid your services will be needed before very long.

(MONYGHAM *takes the cue and grunts sardonically, reverting to his familiar cynical expression.)*

MONYGHAM: The worse people behave, the more I find myself in demand.

INT. BEDROOM IN SOTILLO'S QUARTERS IN ESMERALDA. DAY

Despite the fact that the day is well advanced, SOTILLO *is still sprawled across the huge bed, which at the moment he's sharing with two women. He's startled, not to say indignant, when his aide, a ferocious-looking* MAJOR *like a moustachioed scarecrow, barges into the room and forestalls his protest by thrusting a piece of paper into his hand.*

MAJOR: We intercepted this telegram: I thought you should see it right away.

(SOTILLO *takes the document and tries blearily to focus on it.)*

They're appealing for a boat: until they find one, the silver is sitting in the Customs House. There's anarchy in the town.

SOTILLO: If we decided it was our duty to . . . restore order in Sulaco, how long would it take us to get there?

MAJOR: If we commandeer a steamer, we could be there by midnight.

(SOTILLO *thinks furiously, his eyes narrowed.)*

SOTILLO: We could be in and out with the silver before they knew what hit them.

INT. TELEGRAPH OFFICE AT ESMERALDA. DAY

The sound of splintering, as an axe-head begins to appear through the panel of the locked door.

Through the windows of the telegraph office, a tangle of masts and steamship funnels are visible in Esmeralda harbour. A young TELEGRAPHIST *is crouched intently over his Morse transmitter, furiously tapping. The door panel gives way and a hand reaches in to unlock the door. It's the* MAJOR *who's been wielding the axe and now, to the* TELEGRAPHIST*'s horror, he moves swiftly across the room and brings the axe down on the transmitter, completely* *shattering it.* SOTILLO *has strolled into the room, in the wake of the* MAJOR.

SOTILLO: What message were you sending? And to whom?

TELEGRAPHIST: Just a routine transmission, sir.

(*Silence.* SOTILLO *reflects for a moment. Then he leans to murmur in the* MAJOR*'s ear.*)

SOTILLO: Kill him.

(*The* MAJOR *whips a broad knife out of his belt, throws an arm around the* TELEGRAPHIST *and cuts his throat. In the meantime,* SOTILLO *has turned away and hurried out of the room.*)

EXT. CUSTOMS HOUSE. DAY

The mob bears down on the Customs House, which appears to be entirely deserted. The huge main door is closed and there's no evidence of occupation. The crowd hesitates for a moment, unable to believe its luck, and then surges towards the door.

INT. CUSTOMS HOUSE. DAY

The great hallway is dark, irregularly lit through the narrow windows. GOULD *has moved all his horses and wagons inside the huge space before closing the doors. There's a guard with a Winchester at every window.* GOULD *himself is at a window, one hand in the air, the other holding a revolver.*

INT./EXT. CUSTOMS HOUSE. DAY

GOULD *watches the approach of the mob. He waits until they're very close before bringing his arm down and calling out:*

GOULD: Fire!

(*A volley of rifle-fire. Outside, numbers of rioters collapse.* GOULD *picks his target carefully and squeezes the trigger.*)

EXT. CUSTOMS HOUSE. DAY

The confusion of the mob is intensified by the arrival of NOSTROMO *on his mare, followed by his dockers. Almost at once, demoralized by this double blow, the rioters begin to beat a disorganized retreat.* NOSTROMO *rides over to the entrance of the building.*

INT. CUSTOMS HOUSE. DAY

At GOULD*'s instruction, a couple of his men open the immense door and he steps out.*

EXT. CUSTOMS HOUSE. DAY

GOULD *joins* NOSTROMO*: for a moment they watch the mob, which is in full retreat.*

GOULD: Once again, I'm in your debt.

NOSTROMO: I must go to see my people are safe.

GOULD: I shan't forget this.

(NOSTROMO *nods tersely and rides away.* GOULD *watches him go.*)

INT. LIVING ROOM IN THE ALBERGO D'ITALIA UNA. DAY

The room is lit only by the stripes of brightness admitted by the barred shutters. TERESA VIOLA*'s lips move in silent prayer and* LINDA *and* GISELLE *kneel on either side of her day-bed.* VIOLA *himself sits a little apart from them, under the portrait of Garibaldi, his antiquated rifle across his knees.*

Outside, the mutter of the wind is interrupted by indistinct sounds: distant shouting; hoofbeats; the barking of a dog. All of a sudden a man runs by outside, his shadow blocking the light as he passes; and there's a burst of gunfire. Bullets smack into the wall. VIOLA *rises and cocks his rifle, which makes* TERESA *moan with fear.*

EXT. ALBERGO. DAY

NOSTROMO*, on his horse, fires his Winchester in the direction of the inn. He's engaged a quartet of armed ruffians, who make off when he succeeds in winging one of them in the thigh.*

Once they've scattered, he rides up to the inn, and kicks against the shutter, calling out in Italian.

NOSTROMO: Giorgio! Everyone all right?

(*The shutter is thrown open and* TERESA*'s angry face appears. Dialogue in Italian.*)

TERESA: I asked you not to leave us!

NOSTROMO: It's all right, they've gone. You're safe now.

TERESA: No thanks to you!

(VIOLA *appears beside her in the window, still white with shock.*)

VIOLA: Gian' Battista. I almost shot you. I was about to shoot you.

NOSTROMO: I'm going into town. It's almost over. I'll be back as soon as I can.

(*He wheels his mare and rides away.* TERESA *grips the window-sill, suddenly grey with pain.*)

EXT. CORDILLERA. EVENING

MONTERO *leads his stumbling army down towards the plain, far below, and the distantly glimpsed roofs of Sulaco. There's fairly deep snow on the ground and they're so high up, the red evening sun appears some way below them, illuminating a flock of llamas, grazing on the scrub below.*

INT. AMARILLA CLUB. EVENING

DECOUD *leans on one elbow on the up-ended billiard table looking out across the Plaza Mayor. The room is a mess, littered with spent cartridges, broken glass, bent candlesticks and the odd pool of blood; but the defenders have clearly succeeded in holding out.*

EXT. PLAZA MAYOR. EVENING

His POV*: wisps of smoke curl from the Intendencia, in which not a single window seems to have remained intact. A very old woman, dressed entirely in black, is among the few forlorn figures trudging round the square, inspecting the corpses.*

As DECOUD *watches,* NOSTROMO *rides into the square. The old woman raises a hand in appeal and* NOSTROMO *reins in the mare and leans down to listen to her.*

EXT. PLAZA MAYOR. EVENING

DECOUD *emerges from the Club premises and picks his way between the shattered presses from the* Porvenir *office and a capsized ox-cart with a dead bullock still between the traces. By the time he reaches* NOSTROMO, *the latter has dismounted and hands something to the old woman, who thanks him and moves off, shuffling away across the square.* NOSTROMO *raises a hand to acknowledge* DECOUD.

NOSTROMO: Don Martin.
DECOUD: Who is she?
NOSTROMO: No idea. An old woman looking for her son. She's afraid he may be dead.

(DECOUD *stands next to him for a moment and they look out across the Plaza, contemplating the devastation.*)

DECOUD: You gave her something.
NOSTROMO: Yes. My last quarter-dollar.
DECOUD: Come and have a drink in the club.
NOSTROMO: I don't think they would like that, signor.
DECOUD: What, not even today? When you . . .

(NOSTROMO *shakes his head, his eyes clouded with melancholy. Then he looks up, his attention caught by something: it's* BASILIO *standing at the end of the Calle de la Constitución, waving to them.*)

EXT. PATIO IN THE CASA GOULD. EVENING

OVERHEAD SHOT: NOSTROMO *has tied up his mare under the archway; now he and* DECOUD *follow* BASILIO *into the patio, which has been transformed into something like a field hospital. In one corner,* DR MONYGHAM, *with a couple of female assistants, attends to a wounded man, stretched out on a plain wooden table. Elsewhere, the priest from the Goulds' party is on his knees, taking confession from a dying man; a delegation of Sulaco ladies are tearing strips of linen to make bandages; large numbers of wounded are lying around on straw; and* MRS GOULD *herself is engaged in bandaging a man's chest.*

She's having trouble lifting the man's torso and NOSTROMO *hurries across to take the weight. As soon as she sees who it is,* MRS GOULD*'s face lights up; then she becomes aware of* DECOUD, *hovering uncertainly.*

MRS GOULD: Could you fetch some water, Don Martin?

(*As* DECOUD *moves off, out of earshot,* MRS GOULD *turns back to* NOSTROMO.)

You saved my husband's life today.

NOSTROMO: Perhaps.
MRS GOULD: And not for the first time, I understand.

(MONYGHAM, *watching, is neglecting his patient for the moment, disturbed by the way* NOSTROMO *is smiling at* MRS

GOULD, *acknowledging her thanks. His patient moans and he comes to himself.*

MRS GOULD *ties off the bandage and* NOSTROMO *lowers the man's torso.*)

So you do deserve your reputation.

(DECOUD *arrives with the canister of water he's pumped from the cistern.*)

I think you ought to join my husband upstairs. He may be in need of some support.

(*She turns back to* NOSTROMO, *who by now is supporting the wounded man again, so that* MRS GOULD *can dispense the water.*

DECOUD *turns obediently and moves off towards the broad staircase.*)

EXT. STAIRCASE AND VERANDAH. DAY

DECOUD *reaches the top of the staircase, and looks down at the scene below: the wounded, the bloodstained straw, the way* MRS GOULD *is looking across at* NOSTROMO *in frank admiration, the worried frown of* DR MONYGHAM *as he looks across at them.*

INT. GRAN SALA. EVENING

The great room is lit by the red glow of the setting sun and coated in a layer of dust, and, as DECOUD *appears in the doorway, there's a general movement as all those sitting at the long table turn to look at him. Present are:* GOULD, *somewhat dusty and dishevelled;* DON JOSÉ AVELLANOS, *who has suffered some accident in which half his beard has been burnt away;* ANTONIA, *sitting close to him, concerned at his obvious state of debilitation; and* GAMACHO, *who, supported by a couple of his henchmen, alone seems physically unaffected by the day's events.*

DECOUD: What is the purpose of this meeting?

(*They're surprised by the abruptness of his tone; and it's* GAMACHO *who first formulates an answer, smooth and practised.*)

GAMACHO: Some of us feel that General Montero's democratic aspirations are in many respects legitimate; and for the sake of the preservation of life and property . . .

DECOUD: I see, the purpose of this meeting is surrender.

AVELLANOS: Martin, we are trying to decide how to avoid a bloodbath . . .

(By this time, DECOUD *has arrived at the table. He leans forward to grip the edge of it.)*

DECOUD: And you think the way to do that is to deliver your wives, your children and your property into Montero's hands? Don't you understand? If he prevails, this country goes back into the Dark Ages.

AVELLANOS: Oh, Martin . . .

ANTONIA: You mustn't upset yourself, Father.

(But he looks as if he's about to burst into tears: meanwhile GAMACHO *has risen to his feet, followed a few seconds later by his henchmen.)*

GAMACHO: Your views are well known, Don Martin: but we need practical decisions. We must put the reality of the situation to our various committees and try to arrive at a conclusion not tainted with Conservative selfishness.

DECOUD: Or courage.

(GAMACHO *shoots a look of pure hatred at* DECOUD: *then he storms out of the room, followed by his cronies.* DECOUD *falls into a chair next to* ANTONIA, *who squeezes his hand supportively. He looks across the table at* GOULD.)

Why don't you ask your friends from the north for military assistance?

GOULD: They're businessmen, not soldiers.

DECOUD: Then let them assess the business advantages of a new commercial entity; the independent Republic of Sulaco.

(Silence, as GOULD *considers what to him is a radically new idea.)*

GOULD: Secession?

AVELLANOS: No! How can we allow our country to be broken up?

ANTONIA: Let Martin speak, Father.

DECOUD: If we could offer them a small, manageable country, invasion would be a sound investment, they could finance it with this latest consignment of silver.

GOULD: The silver is sitting in the Customs House.

DECOUD: But Montero will be here by dawn.

GOULD: More serious than that. Our telegraphist received an

unfinished message to the effect that Colonel Sotillo is on his way from Esmeralda and has every intention of stealing it first.

DECOUD: Is there time to get it safely away?

GOULD: Perhaps. I've had a lighter brought over from the harbour. I paid for it myself. All I need is to find someone who can sail it.

DECOUD: I believe the man you want is downstairs.

(GOULD *looks across at him, curious.*)

GOULD: Yes, I think I know who you mean.

EXT. PATIO. EVENING

MONYGHAM *is working on another patient; he looks up, his curiosity intense.*

His POV*: on the other side of the patio,* GOULD *and* DECOUD *are conferring earnestly with* NOSTROMO. MRS GOULD *is nearby, aware of their discussion, but attending to one of the other wounded.*

MONYGHAM *turns reluctantly back to his patient, his mind still elsewhere.*

EXT. APPROACHES TO THE ALBERGO. NIGHT

NOSTROMO *leads his mare by the bridle; and* DECOUD *walks alongside, moving down the dark, rough roadway which leads to the Albergo, the lights of which twinkle not far off.*

NOSTROMO: If I must do such a thing, I would far rather do it alone.

(*Suddenly* LINDA VIOLA *comes racing out of the darkness to intercept them.* GISELLE *is at her heels.*)

LINDA: Gian' Battista! Gian' Battista! Mama is very ill. You must fetch a doctor for her.

(NOSTROMO *hesitates for a second, looking across at* DECOUD.)

DECOUD: We need to set sail within the hour.

GISELLE: Please hurry, Gian' Battista!

(*At this point,* VIOLA, *aware of* NOSTROMO*'s arrival, comes bursting out of the Albergo, calling out in Italian.*)

VIOLA: Gian' Battista! A doctor! For the love of God!

(*Without hesitation,* NOSTROMO *mounts his mare, wheels her round and gallops off into the darkness.* DECOUD *watches him go, concerned, shaking his head at this unexpected turn of events.*)

INT. LIVING-ROOM IN THE ALBERGO. NIGHT

DECOUD *has been shown to a chair at the head of the rough wooden table:* VIOLA *and the two* GIRLS *hover about him.*

VIOLA: You should have something to eat, señor.

DECOUD: No, I'm not hungry: but maybe you could find me some paper?

(*After a moment's puzzlement,* VIOLA *signals to* LINDA *and she brings a pad of plain rough paper from one of the drawers. Then, as* DECOUD *takes it, slips out of his frock-coat, with its pearl-grey silk lining, and hangs it over the back of the chair, finds a pencil in his pocket and leans forward over the pad,* VIOLA *and the* GIRLS *leave him, disappearing up the narrow, curved staircase.*

DECOUD *thinks for a moment. From outside, there's the banshee wail of a steam-whistle and a train clatters by in the night. As it fades into the distance,* DECOUD *writes at the top of the page in bold capitals:*

REPUBLIC OF SULACO
DECLARATION OF INDEPENDENCE

DISSOLVE TO:

DECOUD, *who, having filled several sheets of paper, is now fast asleep, face down on the table.* NOSTROMO *stands above him, touches his shoulder.* DECOUD *wakes with a start and scrambles to his feet.*)

What time is it? We'd better go.

(*As* DECOUD *begins to gather together his pages, fold them, and stuff them in his pocket, he's surprised to see* MRS GOULD *descending the narrow staircase. She looks distressed.*)

MRS GOULD: Teresa is asking to see you, Signor Fidanza.

DECOUD: The silver, Mrs Gould, don't forget the silver.

(MRS GOULD *looks at him sharply. Then she turns to* NOSTROMO.)

MRS GOULD: We'll wait for you.

(*She leaves the room; and* DECOUD *bundles into his frock-coat and follows her out, muttering to* NOSTROMO *as he leaves:*)

DECOUD: Don't be long.

(*More footsteps on the stairs:* MONYGHAM *appears, followed by* VIOLA. MONYGHAM *catches* NOSTROMO*'s eye.*)

MONYGHAM: She wants to see you. Why, I can't imagine. But she's very insistent.

NOSTROMO: She's often like that.

MONYGHAM: Well, I can assure you, she will never be like that again.

(He's spoken harshly to NOSTROMO, *forgetting the presence of* VIOLA, *who now startles him with a quiet question.)*

VIOLA: Is there nothing more to be done for her, Doctor?

(MONYGHAM *avoids his eye and answers gruffly, to conceal a sudden access of emotion.)*

MONYGHAM: Not on this earth.

INT. STAIRCASE IN THE ALBERGO. NIGHT

NOSTROMO *sets off up the stairs reluctantly, approaching an open doorway lit by flickering candles.*

INT. THE VIOLAS' BEDROOM. NIGHT

NOSTROMO *pauses in the doorway, looking down at* TERESA, *who sits up in bed, her head tilted to one side, pain in her eyes.* LINDA *and* GISELLE *sit either side of her. She looks up at* NOSTROMO, *her eyes glittering. Dialogue in Italian.*

TERESA: Their revolutions, you see: this one has killed me.

(NOSTROMO *advances a couple of paces into the room, uncertain. He speaks gently to her.)*

NOSTROMO: I have very little time: what was it you wanted to say to me?

(TERESA *looks at* NOSTROMO *for a moment: then she speaks with some solemnity.)*

TERESA: I want you to promise me that when she is of age, you will marry Linda; and that you will look after the little one as well.

(LINDA *lowers her eyes, then raises them to look directly at* NOSTROMO. GISELLE *is also staring at him, a strange expression on her face. They wait for his answer.)*

NOSTROMO: I promise.

(LINDA *flushes; her eyes sparkle.* TERESA *looks from one daughter to the other.)*

TERESA: And now, my girls, wait downstairs: I have something more to say to Gian' Battista.

(*The* GIRLS *rise reluctantly and leave the room; as their footsteps recede on the staircase,* TERESA *looks up beseechingly at* NOSTROMO.)

Fetch me a priest, Gian' Battista.

NOSTROMO: What?

TERESA: A priest, I need a priest.

(NOSTROMO *stares down at the floor, torn by a dilemma.*)

You refuse a dying woman?

NOSTROMO: They have asked me to save their consignment of silver. It will be the most desperate affair of my life.

TERESA: And what will they give you for it? I'll tell you: a little praise and a stupid name in exchange for your body and your soul.

NOSTROMO: Is it my fault I am the only man capable of this? Would you rather I sold water-melons in the market? You think I should live like a monk? Is that what you want for Linda?

TERESA: You have sold yourself in exchange for their flattery. Your reward will be nothing but misery and despair. And death.

(*She's spoken with great formal intensity, as if pronouncing a curse.* NOSTROMO *looks at her, as if struck dumb.*)

And now go.

(NOSTROMO *backs into the doorway, horror in his eyes. He backs away down the stairs as* TERESA*'s head slumps to one side.*)

EXT. ALBERGO. NIGHT

NOSTROMO *emerges from the Albergo, slipping a poncho over his head.* DECOUD *sits in* MRS GOULD*'s carriage, facing her and the two* VIOLA GIRLS; MRS GOULD *has an arm around each of them.* IGNACIO *is driving the carriage and* BASILIO *rides shotgun, clutching a Winchester across his knees.* MONYGHAM *sits at one of the tables on the restaurant patio and* VIOLA *stands nearby, a glass of wine in his hand, lost in some faraway trance.* NOSTROMO *calls across to* DECOUD.

NOSTROMO: Go!

(MRS GOULD *murmurs to* IGNACIO *and the carriage pulls away. As it vanishes,* NOSTROMO *crosses to embrace* VIOLA.)

Goodbye, old man.

(VIOLA *comes to with a start as* NOSTROMO *touches him.*)
If I don't come back, give the things in my room to Paquita.
(MONYGHAM *looks up at him, smiling his twisted, sardonic smile.*)

MONYGHAM: If you don't come back? I thought Nostromo was infallible.

NOSTROMO: Do you know what they've asked me to do? An impossible task.
(*He strikes a match, lights his cigar and holds the match up, watching the unwavering flame.*)
And look: no wind. Not even a breath of wind. And no moon. Still, one must do one's duty.
(VIOLA, *still next to him, looks up and speaks, calmly and quietly, as if stating a most obvious truth.*)

VIOLA: The rich, you know, Gian' Battista, they keep us as they keep dogs, to fight and hunt in their service.
(NOSTROMO *looks at him, his expression defensive.*)

NOSTROMO: If I succeed, my name will live forever.

MONYGHAM: Is that a good bargain?

NOSTROMO: What bargain would you have made?

MONYGHAM: I'll tell you: for taking that curse on my back, nothing less than the whole treasure would do.
(*He's looking straight at* NOSTROMO, *his eyes narrowed and his expression cold.* NOSTROMO*'s jaw sets, he mounts his mare and gallops away into the night.*)

EXT. LIGHTER, NIGHT

The silver has been stacked amidships, forming a kind of floor just below the water-line, emitting a kind of eerie glow. NOSTROMO*'s bare feet move across it and spring back on to dry land.*

EXT. JETTY. NIGHT

There's a group of people with lanterns on the little jetty behind the looming Customs House: MRS GOULD *sits in her landau, with* LINDA *and* GISELLE VIOLA*;* GOULD, *impassively smoking a cigar, stands nearby; and* DECOUD *is slightly off to one side with* ANTONIA, *who has tears in her eyes.*

ANTONIA: You will be careful.

(*He takes her in his arms and kisses her tears away; but suddenly* NOSTROMO *is at his elbow.*)

NOSTROMO: We are ready, signor.

(DECOUD *acknowledges him, kisses* ANTONIA *again. Meanwhile,* GOULD *steps out of the shadows to approach* NOSTROMO.)

GOULD: This time you won't find me ungrateful. Good luck.

(*He pumps* NOSTROMO*'s hand. Meanwhile* DECOUD *is extricating himself with some difficulty from* ANTONIA*'s embrace.*)

ANTONIA: I'll always love you.

DECOUD: Goodbye.

(NOSTROMO *is moving back towards the boat, when* LINDA *suddenly jumps down from the landau and rushes to intercept him. She buries herself in his arms, as* GISELLE *steps down from the carriage herself.*)

LINDA: Gian' Battista!

(*She reaches up for him and awkwardly, but passionately, gives him what must almost certainly be her first adult kiss.* GISELLE *watches, obviously very affected. Then, when* LINDA *releases* NOSTROMO *at last, she darts in to give him an embarrassed peck on the cheek. The look they exchange after this has some strange and powerful undercurrent. Then, abruptly,* NOSTROMO *turns away.* DECOUD, *meanwhile, has said his goodbyes and shaken hands with everyone; and joins* NOSTROMO *as he descends the steps of the jetty and springs aboard the lighter.*)

EXT. LIGHTER. NIGHT

From the POV *of the spectators on the jetty:* DECOUD *stands watching* NOSTROMO, *as he uses a heavy oar to push away from land.*

EXT. JETTY. NIGHT

GOULD *glances up at the star-filled sky, concerned, then returns his attention to the lighter.*

EXT. LIGHTER. NIGHT

NOSTROMO *ships the oar and hurries aft to hoist the mainsail.*

EXT. JETTY. NIGHT

CLOSE *on* ANTONIA, *tears rolling down her cheeks.*

EXT. LIGHTER. NIGHT

From the POV *of the spectators, the lighter begins to edge away into the darkness. The sail flaps briefly as the wind gusts and dies.* DECOUD *raises an arm and calls out bravely:*

DECOUD: *Au revoir*! When next we meet it will be in the Republic of Sulaco!

EXT. JETTY. NIGHT

GOULD *now stands alongside* MRS GOULD *and the* VIOLA GIRLS, *a kind of grim satisfaction in his expression.* MRS GOULD*'s attention is focused on the two* GIRLS, *both of whom are crying. Then she looks up to watch the disappearing boat.*

EXT. LIGHTER. NIGHT

CLOSE *on* DECOUD: *his confidence visibly evaporating as the reality of the situation begins to dawn on him.*

His POV*: the jetty is receding into a distant pool of light.*

EXT. GOLFO PLACIDO. NIGHT

The lighter is now only visible as a silhouette against the stars. It glides away into the darkness, as silent as if it is launching into space.

EXT. LIGHTER. NIGHT

Silence and darkness. Then, minuscule sounds begin to be heard; the ripple of water, the creak of timbers, the slap of canvas, the groan of rope. The blackness is breached by two commas of greenish light. Soon, it becomes clear that these form the phosphorescent bow wave of the lighter as it labours forward. NOSTROMO *is a dark outline at the helm, silhouetted against the dazzling array of stars, dimly lit from below.*

The light-source is the silver itself, reflecting the starlight and dully glowing as if from within.

NOSTROMO: We are out in the Gulf.

DECOUD: Yes. No one can find us now.

(*He's forward of* NOSTROMO, *scarcely visible, looking out*

across the surface of the water, awed by the solitude.
The mast-head moves slowly across huge clusters of stars.
DECOUD *starts as a match flares astern.* NOSTROMO *is examining the compass. The sounds have faded.* NOSTROMO *leans forward and makes a strange chirruping, to encourage the breeze.* DECOUD *watches, fascinated. Then, he looks up.*
The mast-head now appears to be stationary.)
Do we move at all?
NOSTROMO: Slower than a beetle tangled in the grass.

EXT. GOLFO PLACIDO. NIGHT
The blade of a great oar plunges into the still water, disrupting the reflection of the stars and causing dancing phosphorescent ripples.

EXT. LIGHTER. NIGHT
NOSTROMO *and* DECOUD *stand, port and starboard, operating the huge oars. Behind them, the sail hangs limp.* NOSTROMO *grunts impatiently.*
NOSTROMO: Pull. We are making a crooked path.
(DECOUD *does his best to respond, but he's clearly exhausted.*)
Anybody would think this was the last consignment of silver in the world. Why did Don Carlos have to tie it around my neck?
DECOUD: He didn't want it falling into the wrong hands.
NOSTROMO: It won't. I have an axe on board and I shall cut a hole below the water-line and let the sea have the treasure, before I give it up.
(DECOUD *heaves painfully on his oar.*)

EXT. GOLFO PLACIDO. NIGHT
As the blade of the oar rises from the water, the phosphorescence dances and twinkles eerily.
DECOUD: (*Off-screen*) Look. The sea is already full of silver.

EXT. LIGHTER. NIGHT
DECOUD *stoops to complete another punishing stroke.*
NOSTROMO: Tonight I refused to fetch a priest for a dying woman. She must have died thinking I deprived her of Paradise.

(DECOUD *is really struggling now: he tries to make his tone as casual as possible.*)

DECOUD: We're in no great hurry, are we?

NOSTROMO: Rest your arms for a while, signor, if that's what you mean.

(DECOUD *hauls in his oar with a little sigh of relief and flops back, his legs stretched out across the silver. He looks ruefully at his red and blistered hands.* NOSTROMO, *meanwhile, settles by the tiller, his arms clasped around his knees. After a time, he cocks his head to one side, listening.*)

What's the matter, Don Martin?

DECOUD: What?

NOSTROMO: Are you all right?

DECOUD: Yes. Why?

(NOSTROMO *strikes a match and lights a stump of candle; then he moves swiftly over to* DECOUD *and holds the candle up to illuminate the latter's face.*)

NOSTROMO: I could have sworn I could hear somebody weeping.

(*The ensuing silence is broken by the unmistakable sound of a stifled sob from somewhere forward.* NOSTROMO *hands* DECOUD *the candle-end and moves forward, flitting swiftly across the silver. He crouches low and grasps beneath the half-deck. He stiffens as his hand comes into contact with something. He reaches in under the deck and drags out a man, by his hair and coat-collar. He sends him sprawling across the pile of silver, where it becomes noticeable that he's missing a shoe.*

NOSTROMO *takes back his candle-end and holds it to the man's face: it's* HIRSCH, *battered and dusty, grey with terror, his eyes tightly closed.* DECOUD *reaches forward and shakes his rigid body.*)

DECOUD: Who are you? What do you think you're doing?

NOSTROMO: He's dead. Let's throw him overboard.

(*One of* HIRSCH*'s eyes opens. He utters a soft and miserable groan.*)

HIRSCH: No.

(NOSTROMO *drags* HIRSCH *up into a sitting position.*)

NOSTROMO: Now. Explain yourself.

HIRSCH: Water.

(*His appeal is so abject and quavering that* DECOUD *reaches at once for one of the water cans, which he uncaps and holds to* HIRSCH*'s lips.* HIRSCH *swallows avidly, water running down over his chin. Eventually, with a kind of shuddering sigh, he pushes the can away.*)

My name is Hirsch. I am only a small businessman.

DECOUD: We are not open for business.

HIRSCH: I was hiding from the riots. I thought this would be a safe place.

NOSTROMO: Why were you making that noise?

HIRSCH: I heard you say you would sink the boat. I can't swim.

NOSTROMO: All right. Get back where you were.

(HIRSCH *scuttles off into the darkness with extraordinary agility. There's the sound of a heavy fall; then a small, scrabbling noise.*)

And keep still. If I so much as hear you breathe too loud, I shall come forward and kill you.

(*After a moment,* DECOUD *whispers to* NOSTROMO.)

DECOUD: He seems harmless.

NOSTROMO: No. There is no room for fear in this lighter.

(*He moves away, back to the tiller. He consults the compass, tucks the tiller under his arm and pinches out the candle.*

DECOUD*'s head goes up in the darkness: he's heard a strange scurrying whisper, approaching across the surface of the water.*)

DECOUD: What's that?

NOSTROMO: Rain. Rain on the water.

(*The sound approaches: eerie, feathery as a flight of arrows.*)

EXT. GOLFO PLACIDO. NIGHT

The rain spreads fast across the water, throwing up countless needles of phosphorescence.

EXT. LIGHTER. NIGHT

As the rain approaches, it lights the outlines of DECOUD *and* NOSTROMO. *It crashes over the boat and* DECOUD *turns his face up into the shower. There's a muffled crack as the sail fills with wind.* NOSTROMO *begins to make adjustments to the tiller.*

EXT. GOLFO PLACIDO. NIGHT

The lighter, its sail bellying out for a moment, begins to make some progress, its shape etched against the night sky, phosphorescence flashing at its bows.

Then, in an instant, the shower has passed and can be seen and heard retreating across the surface of the sea, until silence falls once again.

EXT. LIGHTER. NIGHT

DECOUD *shakes the glistening drops out of his hair. Then he stops, hearing another sound.* NOSTROMO*'s listening too, alert as a whippet.*

DECOUD: Here comes another.

(*He listens: but the sound is somehow different from before, heavier, like horses in snow.* NOSTROMO *shakes his head slowly.*)

NOSTROMO: No. That's not rain.

DECOUD: What do you mean?

NOSTROMO: That's a steamer.

(*The whites of* DECOUD*'s eyeballs gleam in alarm.*)

EXT. GOLFO PLACIDO. NIGHT

The reflections of the stars tremble on the surface of the water, as the sound gradually becomes identifiable as the throb and splutter of a large propeller.

EXT. LIGHTER. NIGHT

DECOUD *moves aft until he's close to* NOSTROMO. *Their heads rise, pale, on either side of the tiller.*

NOSTROMO: She's carrying no lights. Must be the steamer from Esmeralda.

(NOSTROMO, *instinctively crouches down below the gunwale and* DECOUD *follows suit. They speak in whispers.*)

I should have killed that man.

DECOUD: Yes.

NOSTROMO: But once I saw you giving him the water, I couldn't do it.

EXT. GOLFO PLACIDO. NIGHT

The steamer is coming closer and closer, but the night is still impenetrably black. By the sound of it, the ship is now almost upon them.

EXT. LIGHTER. NIGHT

NOSTROMO *leans forward to breathe into* DECOUD*'s ear.*

NOSTROMO: Don't move. The slightest sound may cost us our lives. I'm going to lower the sail.

(He starts to inch forward; but freezes when, all of a sudden, the ship's engines cut out with a great hiss of steam. He peers out into the silence of the night.)

EXT. GOLF PLACIDO. NIGHT

NOSTROMO*'s* POV*: however close the steamer may be, it remains quite invisible.*

EXT. LIGHTER. NIGHT

NOSTROMO *moves stealthily forward, wary as a cat.* DECOUD *watches him; then his head jerks up in shock.*

What he's seen is an approaching cloud of steam. It drifts slowly through the shrouds. Suddenly, DECOUD*'s enveloped in it.*

NOSTROMO*, steam swirling around him, begins with infinite care to lower the sail. Strange sounds from the steamer echo resonantly across the water: footsteps on deck, the occasional exchange of orders, the groan and clank of metal, all apparently happening no more than a few yards away.*

DECOUD *watches as the sail is lowered, revealing more and more stars and a distant bank of silver cloud.*

HIRSCH*'s head moves cautiously out of the darkness like a tortoise emerging from its shell. His eyes are wide with terror.*

NOSTROMO *completes his task, lowering the yard on the deck as if it were made of glass.*

A curtain of fine rain drifts across the boat. Then, suddenly, the sharp sound of a ship's bell. The steamer's engines start up again, a deep, throbbing roar, very nearby. The two men look at each other.

EXT. GOLFO PLACIDO. NIGHT

Heavy rain again: it sweeps across the water and the phosphorescence sparkles.

EXT. LIGHTER. NIGHT

NOSTROMO *and* DECOUD, *their features highlighted by the phosphorescence, strain to see something as the rain splashes down, perpendicular. The sound of the steamer's propeller and engines increases to a roar.*

EXT. GOLFO PLACIDO. NIGHT

Shouted orders ring out across the water, through the rain: the clicks and rattles of equipment seem close enough to touch, but still nothing is to be seen.

EXT. LIGHTER. NIGHT

HIRSCH*'s terrified face rises into frame, his chin on a level with the foredeck. Suddenly his eyes widen in horror and disbelief.*

EXT. GOLFO PLACIDO. NIGHT

Looming out of the darkness, lit by the phosphorescent rain, only yards away, is the mountainous prow of the steamer.

EXT. LIGHTER. NIGHT

NOSTROMO *and* DECOUD *rise in the foreground, as the steamer towers above them.*

It bears down on the lighter, seen through the silhouette of the rigging.

HIRSCH*'s mouth opens wide, but no sound emerges.*

The blunt prow of the steamer collides obliquely with the lighter, aft of the bowsprit.

There's a splintering of wood. NOSTROMO *and* DECOUD *are thrown sideways by the force of the collision.* HIRSCH *is hurled back against the side of the lighter, as water begins to pour in over the bulwarks.*

The grinding scrape of steel against timber, as the prow of the steamer runs along the side of the lighter, tipping it over at a dangerous angle.

Operating entirely by instinct, HIRSCH *manages to scramble up from the swirling foamy water and back on to the foredeck.*

NOSTROMO *and* DECOUD *are also trying to pick themselves up, as the water sweeps down the deck and engulfs them.*

HIRSCH *throws his arms around the mast and clings on for dear life. He looks up, panic in his eyes.*

Above his head, the steamer's anchor moves towards him. It's about eight feet above the surface of the sea. As the steamer proceeds, one of the anchor flukes catches in one of the wire shrouds attached to the mast; and for a moment the entire lighter is being dragged along backwards.

HIRSCH *groans in terror as the mast bends under the strain.*

DECOUD, *astern, watches in astonishment as* HIRSCH *scrambles up on the fluke. No sooner has he done so than the shroud snaps and the anchor springs away, carrying* HIRSCH *with it.*

NOSTROMO *grabs the tiller, as the lighter rights itself. He sees* HIRSCH, *carried away on the anchor, yelling incoherently. As* DECOUD *moves over to him, the long, black side of the steamer passes out of frame. Somewhere out of the darkness comes a distant banshee wail.*

NOSTROMO: He's a dead man.

(*The steamer's propeller, churning up a maelstrom of phosphorescence, dwindles away into the blackness of the night.*)

INT. SOTILLO'S QUARTERS IN THE CUSTOMS HOUSE. DAWN

SOTILLO *is sitting in a chair with one highly-polished boot placed on the rump of a sweating sergeant, who is struggling to remove the other.* SOTILLO *pushes hard and the boot comes off.*

SOTILLO *has installed himself in the room where once the rifles were stored. His hat, sword and revolver lie on the desk. A net hammock has been slung in one corner of the room. The pink light of dawn peeps through the jalousies.*

Beside him stands the homicidal MAJOR. SOTILLO *flexes his toes and looks up at him. Finally he murmurs:*

SOTILLO: All right. Bring him in.

EXT. ISLAND OF GREAT ISABEL. DAY

The lighter bobs, half-aground on the little beach at the foot of a small ravine in the shadow of a cliff on the landward side of the island. Long gashes in the wood and buckled metal show the results of the collision. The silver is no longer amidships.

In the shadow of the single gnarled and twisted tree, NOSTROMO *finishes flattening out an area of sand with a long shovel.* DECOUD, *whose frock-coat and cravat hang from the branches, has already dropped his shovel and is leaning against the tree, obviously quite exhausted.* NOSTROMO *drops his shovel and flops down next to* DECOUD.

A WIDER SHOT *reveals an idyllic scene. Butterflies dance in the pellucid air above a clear stream, which ebbs away in the sand of the beach. The transparent green water of the cove is striped with vivid yellow seaweed, waving just below the surface. A grapnel secures the lighter to the thick roots of a shrub. The lighter's dinghy has been hauled up into the bushes, so that it's not visible from the sea; it's stacked with various boxes of provisions.*

DECOUD *looks up from rueful contemplation of the ragged red blisters on his palms.*

DECOUD: I suppose this must be life, since it is so much like a dream.

(NOSTROMO *makes no response to this observation;* DECOUD *casts about for something more concrete to say.*)

Landing us here was a stroke of genius.

NOSTROMO: This is the island of Great Isabel, signor. I once spent a whole Sunday exploring every inch of it.

DECOUD: Misanthropic sort of occupation.

NOSTROMO: It was near the end of the month. I had no money. (*He reaches for a pebble and throws it down into the stream below.*) The water in that stream is very sweet.

DECOUD: I'm pleased to hear it.

NOSTROMO: And you have two weeks' food there in the dinghy.

DECOUD: You know, once Montero has arrived, I can't go back to the mainland.

NOSTROMO: You will be safe here, signor. Nobody will come. The people of this country are not curious. (*He rises to his feet, businesslike once again; and treads down an irregularity in the sand, where the silver is buried.*) And the silver. The silver will be safe for hundreds of years. It is incorruptible.

DECOUD: As some men are said to be.

NOSTROMO: I do not always understand what you mean, Don

Martin. I know all this would have been much simpler if you had not been with me.

DECOUD: Without me to pump, you would have gone to the bottom.

NOSTROMO: Yes . . . alone.

EXT. BEACH. DAY

DECOUD *stands knee-deep in the sea, the island rising behind him.*

REVERSE SHOT: DECOUD *is watching* NOSTROMO *scramble aboard the lighter as it glides smoothly away into deep water.*

CLOSE *on* DECOUD: *he's trying to look calm and cheerful, but his eyes are full of panic.*

Aboard the lighter, NOSTROMO *takes the tiller and shouts back to* DECOUD.

NOSTROMO: Stay down in the ravine. I'll try to come out to you in a night or two.

(DECOUD, *seen from his* POV, *a receding figure, forlorn among the seaweed. He raises a hand in farewell.*)

EXT. LIGHTER. DAY

NOSTROMO *brings down his axe, chopping cleanly through the bottom of the lighter. Water floods in and swirls around his ankles. He springs lightly up on to the taffrail, pauses for a moment, then dives cleanly into the sea.*

EXT. ISLAND OF GREAT ISABEL. DAY

DECOUD *is still standing knee-deep in the water, looking out to sea. Some distance away, half-way to the mainland, the lighter is sinking. The sail is the last part of it to disappear, suddenly sucked under by some vicious submarine force. Now only the sea is visible and the great range of mountains rearing above Sulaco.*

CLOSE *on* DECOUD: *he slowly lowers the hand that's been shading his eyes. Suddenly, he's overwhelmingly aware of his own isolation, genuinely frightened for perhaps the first time in his life.*

FADE

EXT. ROCKY COVE. DAY

NOSTROMO *is asleep in the shade of a deserted cove. Above him is a kind of cairn, a simple grave marked by a plain bronze cross.*

A shadow passes over the beach and a black vulture, an ugly creature with a naked red neck, lands on the cross and settles down to wait, watching NOSTROMO, *who hasn't stirred, his mouth open, his cheek pressed against the rock.*

EXT. CATHEDRAL BELFRY. DAY

The giant bell in the belfry begins to toll, sounding a deep and sinister note.

HIGH ANGLE LONG SHOT: *far below, an unidentifiable* GENERAL MONTERO, *on horseback, is leading his ragtag army, all of them on foot, in through the gates of the deserted town.*

Gradually, more bells begin to chime: until every bell in the town has combined in a furious exultant clangour.

INT. GRAN SALA IN THE CASA GOULD. DAY

GOULD, MRS GOULD *and* MONYGHAM *are all at table; and all transfixed by the thunderous sound of the bells. After a while,* GOULD *turns to the quaking* BASILIO *and speaks, an edge of irritation in his voice.*

GOULD: Shut the windows.

(BASILIO *hurries to do as he's told, slamming the first window shut in his haste.*)

EXT. PLAZA MAYOR. DAY

A CLOSE TRACKING SHOT *follows* MONTERO, *gaunt as a scarecrow, his carefully preserved cocked hat contrasting with the battered remains of his uniform.*

Behind him his emaciated troops trudge into the square, a torrent of rubbish in a cloud of dust, filthy and exhausted, the majority barefoot, moving to the beating of drums. The local populace can be glimpsed behind windows, in side-alleys, but most people have decided to give the conquerors a wide berth.

EXT. INTENDENCIA. DAY

GAMACHO, *surrounded by a dozen or so nervous-looking officials, stands on the steps outside the sacked Intendencia, with its smashed windows and charred façade, making last-minute adjustments to his chain of office.*

EXT. ISLAND OF GREAT ISABEL. DAY

DECOUD *is listening. He moves down the ravine towards the beach. Very faintly, across the waters of the gulf, comes the sound of the bells. He shakes his head, troubled.*

EXT. CUSTOMS HOUSE. DAY

CLOSE *on* SOTILLO, *who is visibly agitated, hearing the sound of the bells. He stands by the open door of the Customs House, a phalanx of troops visible in the great entrance hall behind him. He mutters to the* MAJOR.

SOTILLO: Move everybody out. We're going back on board the steamer.

(*The* MAJOR *makes a gesture in the direction of* SOTILLO*'s quarters.*)

MAJOR: What about . . . ?

(SOTILLO *interrupts him with a curt nod.*)

SOTILLO: When we leave, burn the place down.

EXT. INTENDENCIA. DAY

Seen from over GAMACHO*'s shoulder,* MONTERO *urges his horse slowly and deliberately up the steps of the Intendencia, until he towers over* GAMACHO, *a colossal, menacing figure.* GAMACHO *spreads his arms in a welcoming gesture, but* MONTERO *completely ignores him, rides by and disappears, still on horseback, through the broad doorway of the building, his expression stony.*

EXT. COURTYARD OF THE INTENDENCIA. DAY

MONTERO, *impassive, rides across the large courtyard to the wooden staircase in the corner.* GAMACHO *and his officials hurry through the doorway. For a moment they can't see* MONTERO*: then* GAMACHO *looks up, his eyes popping.*

His POV*:* MONTERO *is riding along the verandah which leads off the staircase.*

INT. GRAN SALA IN THE CASA GOULD. DAY

A striking tableau: against one wall, fearfully huddled in rigid silence, is the entire domestic household of the Casa Gould: old men and women; virtually naked children; maids, liveried staff and obscure labourers, all standing shoulder to shoulder. MRS GOULD

and MONYGHAM *are still at the table,* GOULD *is on his feet.*
All of a sudden, the bells stop. GOULD *looks up, frowning. There's a moment's stillness and then* BASILIO *bustles into the room.*

BASILIO: Don Carlos: General Montero has sent for you.

GOULD: Very well.

(*He moves swiftly towards the double-doors. Some of the women cross themselves.* MRS GOULD, *pale, has risen to her feet.* DR MONYGHAM *arrives at her elbow and takes her arm as* GOULD *leaves the room.*)

EXT. COURTYARD IN THE INTENDENCIA. DAY

An escort of four soldiers marches GOULD *into the courtyard. Groups of civilians wait disconsolately, some under armed guard.* MONTERO*'s soldiers, still ravaged but with the insolence of victory, lounge about, smoking. And most striking of all, a group of civilians is being led to the immense whitewashed wall and made to stand against it. As* GOULD *is hustled up the wooden staircase to the verandah above, a ragged volley rings out and the half-dozen victims collapse untidily, leaving smears of blood on the whitewash.* GOULD*'s expression remains icy calm.*

INT. INTENDENCIA. DAY

The room in which GOULD *was once interviewed by* GAMACHO *still has all the signs of the mob's destructive invasion.* MONTERO *sits at a trestle table, on a plain, wooden chair, unshaven, eyes sunken in his fearsome profile, looking across at a cool and self-possessed* GOULD.

GOULD: Your cable arrived just too late to prevent the export of the silver. Most unfortunate.

(MONTERO *seems unaffected by this news; he smiles wolfishly.*)

MONTERO: Can't be helped, Don Carlos: and after all, what is one consignment?

GOULD: Quite.

MONTERO: No, until the war is brought to its successful conclusion, it will be my patriotic duty to commandeer the mine itself.

GOULD: I'm afraid I can't allow that.

(MONTERO, *a little rattled by* GOULD*'s impassivity, rises and makes his way over to the window.*)

MONTERO: I'm not offering you a choice in the matter.

(MONTERO *opens the window and looks down at the Plaza below. There's the sound of cheering.*)

EXT. PLAZA MAYOR. DAY

MONTERO*'s* POV*:* GAMACHO*, standing on an improvised platform, is addressing a large and enthusiastic crowd.*

GAMACHO: France, England, Germany, the United States!

INT. INTENDENCIA. DAY

MONTERO *watches;* GAMACHO*'s* VOICE *floats up from below.*

GAMACHO: (*Off-screen*) They are all our enemies, fellow citizens, exploiters of our country. And with our new democracy behind us, we shall declare war on them all!

(*Another cheer goes up, and* MONTERO *turns back into the room.*)

MONTERO: This Gamacho. He seems very . . . popular.

GOULD: He is well-liked.

MONTERO: He is?

GOULD: He receives a salary from the mine. As, I need hardly remind you, does every minister in the government.

MONTERO: And did he issue your export licence?

GOULD: He did.

(MONTERO *turns to an* AIDE*, who has been lurking aimlessly over by the door. He speaks to him loudly, the subtext of his remarks aimed squarely at* GOULD*.*)

MONTERO: Allow Señor Gamacho to complete his oration, however many hours it may take.

AIDE: Yes, Your Excellency.

MONTERO: Then arrest him; and, as soon as is convenient, have him garrotted.

(*The* AIDE *bows and leaves the room.* MONTERO *grins at* GOULD*.*)

I know I can count on your full co-operation as regards the mine.

(GOULD *returns his gaze evenly, quite unmoved.*)

GOULD: I am certainly open to negotiation.

MONTERO: You will not find me ungrateful. A title, perhaps? How would you like to be the Count of Sulaco?

GOULD: I don't think I've made myself quite clear. European investment in this country, the next instalment of the American loan, business confidence throughout the world, all depend upon the smooth functioning of the San Tomé mine. And I will not renounce my control of it in any particular. You may of course have me killed, as well. But all you will achieve is the destruction of the mine and the collapse of your country's economy.

(MONTERO *is at a loss for a reply. Stalemate.*)

EXT. VERANDAH IN THE CASA GOULD. DAY

MRS GOULD *is pacing up and down, trying very hard to control her anxiety. Facing her, in an armchair so placed that his face is in shadow, is* DR MONYGHAM.

MRS GOULD: A man like Montero: I don't know how he can bring himself to look any of his old acquaintances in the eye.

MONYGHAM: He'll no doubt get over the first awkwardness by having some of them shot. Nothing suits your military man who has changed sides so well as a few summary executions. (*He sits up hastily, suddenly aware of his tactlessness.*) Not that he'd dare harm your husband. (*He sinks back in his chair, troubled.*)

MRS GOULD: You were here when all this happened before, weren't you? During the purge?

MONYGHAM: Yes. (*He stares ahead of him, unseeing.*)

INT. PRISON CELL. DAY

It's twenty years earlier. DR MONYGHAM, *sitting on the floor of a cramped and filthy cell, unfurnished except for a bucket, looks up at the sound of approaching footsteps. A fleeting image.*

EXT. VERANDAH. DAY

CLOSE *on* DR MONYGHAM, *as he dismisses the memory from his mind.*

MONYGHAM: Yes, I was.

(*In an effort to shake himself free of these thoughts, he rises and hobbles over to the banister, staring unseeingly down into the patio.* MRS GOULD *watches him, concerned.*)

MRS GOULD: And didn't they arrest you?

(MONYGHAM *stands with his back to her, unmoving.*)

INT. PRISON CELL. DAY

The cell door is unlocked and thrown open. Standing in the doorway, towering over MONYGHAM, *is a tall, overweight, unshaven priest with a stained cassock embellished with military decorations:* FATHER BERON. *Behind him are four men in uniform.*

BERON: It's time for confession.

EXT. VERANDAH. DAY

DR MONYGHAM *looks haunted and ill;* MRS GOULD *is troubled by his obvious distress.*

MRS GOULD: Do sit down, doctor.

(*Without answering,* MONYGHAM *returns to his armchair and slumps into it.*)

INT. INTERROGATION CHAMBER. DAY

MONYGHAM, *in chains, sits on a stool in a spacious stone room like the refectory in a monastery, facing a tribunal consisting of four officers. Seated at one end of the table is* FATHER BERON.

CLOSE *on* MONYGHAM. *A grubby strip of bandage passes across his nose and covers wounds on both cheeks. He shakes his head, miserable but defiant.*

BERON: This is a waste of time. (*Carefully, he lays down his quill pen.*) Let me take him outside. (*He reaches under the table and produces a heavy wooden mallet.*)

EXT. VERANDAH. DAY

DR MONYGHAM *opens his eyes. He looks across at* MRS GOULD, *his expression suddenly belligerent.*

MONYGHAM: They told you I was arrested, did they?

MRS GOULD: Yes.

MONYGHAM: And did they tell you I betrayed all my friends? Every single one.

(MRS GOULD *hesitates: then she turns her candid gaze on him.*)

MRS GOULD: I have heard something of the sort. Naturally, I didn't believe a word of it.

(MONYGHAM *softens at once. For a moment he looks at her*

with undisguised emotion. Eventually, he speaks, moved.)

MONYGHAM: Thank you. (*Then he looks away, a harder edge entering his voice.*) Nevertheless, it's true.

MRS GOULD: Then they must have driven you beyond endurance.

MONYGHAM: They did.

INT. TORTURE ROOM. DAY

CLOSE *on* MONYGHAM. *Dark scabs disfigure his cheeks. A worn leather strap across his chest pinions him to a grimy table. His mouth is stopped with a leather gag. He turns his face and nods feebly.*

ANOTHER ANGLE *gives a fleeting impression of* FATHER BERON *leaning in to undo the gag. The mallet leans against the wall.* MONYGHAM*'s trousers are drenched with blood.*

VERY CLOSE *now, as* MONYGHAM*'s lips begin to move next to* FATHER BERON*'s ear: an image of the confessional.*

EXT. VERANDAH. DAY

DR MONYGHAM*'s face, as he struggles with his memories. He looks up at* MRS GOULD.

MONYGHAM: Strangely enough, there's only one thing I can never forgive. He let me live.

(MRS GOULD *is looking at him; finally, she speaks, tenderly.*)

MRS GOULD: Who?

MONYGHAM: His name was Father Beron. He's been dead for years. Doesn't stop me expecting to see him round every street corner. And never a week goes by without my dreaming he's coming for me.

(*He breaks off.* MRS GOULD*'s eyes are full of understanding. Suddenly, however, she's distracted by the sound of footsteps down below in the patio. She jumps up.*)

EXT. PATIO AND STAIRCASE. DAY

GOULD *strides across the patio. He's so preoccupied, he doesn't see the others above. Instead he barks at the hovering* BASILIO.

GOULD: Have my horse saddled at once.

(*By now,* MRS GOULD *is hurrying down the stairs towards him.*)

MRS GOULD: You're safe.

(GOULD *doesn't answer, instead he speaks almost as if to himself.*)

GOULD: That common criminal means to take the mine.

MRS GOULD: What will you do?

GOULD: Organize its defence. Set the dynamite.

(*By now,* MONYGHAM *has hobbled down the stairs to join them.*)

MONYGHAM: You're prepared to destroy it?

GOULD: If necessary.

(MONYGHAM *shakes his head disapprovingly.*)

What we need is for someone to go over the mountains and bring back Barrios. He and the rifles are probably our only hope. Pity that Italian shipped out with the silver.

MONYGHAM: Surely we can find someone else.

GOULD: We have about a week's grace. Montero's men are exhausted; and if we can keep Sotillo's soldiers from joining forces with them, that may buy us a little longer.

MONYGHAM: Perhaps I could help.

GOULD: How?

MONYGHAM: If I were to convince Sotillo that the silver was still somewhere in the town, wouldn't that divert his energies?

(GOULD *looks at him, assessing the idea: finally, he speaks.*)

GOULD: Yes, you may be right.

(BASILIO *leads the horse over to* GOULD: *he takes the reins and swings up into the saddle.*)

He's in the Customs House. Good luck.

(*He wheels his horse.* MRS GOULD *raises a hand in farewell, but he ignores her, spurs his horse and disappears back into the street.* MRS GOULD *turns to* MONYGHAM.)

MRS GOULD: It seems too dangerous.

MONYGHAM: He knows how to look after himself.

MRS GOULD: No, Doctor, I mean what you're suggesting.

(MONYGHAM *is so overwhelmed by the realization that she's concerned for him, he is momentarily at a loss.* MRS GOULD *reaches out impulsively and takes both his hands.*)

Aren't you running a terrible risk?

(*Her eyes are full of tears.* MONYGHAM *collects himself sufficiently to remove his hands and assume his familiar bantering tone.*)

MONYGHAM: I know you'll defend my memory.

(*He turns abruptly and limps out of the patio, leaving* MRS GOULD *alone and troubled.*)

EXT. GOLFO PLACIDO. SUNSET

A brilliantly red sun moves down to meet the waters of the Gulf.

EXT. ROCKY COVE. SUNSET

NOSTROMO *is still asleep. The sun is moving so fast, we see a shadow moving across his face. When the sun shines into his eyes, they open to see:*

The vulture, still waiting patiently on top of the cross. As he stirs, it jumps down on to the ground.

NOSTROMO *sits up, abruptly. The vulture back-pedals in sudden alarm, its bare red neck jerking agitatedly.* NOSTROMO *jumps to his feet and bears down on it, waving his arms. The vulture lumbers into its clumsy take-off and soars away into the sky.*

NOSTROMO: I'm not dead yet.

(*He stands in the lurid glare of sunset, his expression uncharacteristically uncertain. Then, looking down the coast towards the harbour, he comes to a decision and sets off, running, barefoot, along the beach.*)

EXT. SEASHORE. SUNSET

NOSTROMO *flits along the shore, between the dark palm groves and the flat sheet of the sea, in the last garish blaze of sunset. He runs automatically, but his face is working as memories begin to sweep over him. From somewhere on the plain comes the mournful hooting of an owl.*

TERESA: (*Voice-over in Italian*) And what will they give you for it? A little praise and a stupid name in exchange for your body and your soul.

NOSTROMO: *Siempre* Nostromo!

(*His voice, ringing out in the quiet of the evening, sets off a chorus of barking dogs from a broken-down Indian settlement.*

He swerves to take a short-cut through the palm grove.)

EXT. PALM-GROVE. EVENING

The sun has set now and the swift tropical night is falling.

NOSTROMO *runs on, trying to escape the pursuing voices.*

MONYGHAM: (*Voice-over*) . . . for taking that curse on my back, nothing less than the whole treasure would do.

(NOSTROMO *runs the back of his hand across his eyes, clearing the sweat.*)

viola: (*Voice-over*) The rich, you know, Gian' Battista, they keep us as they keep dogs, to fight and hunt in their service.

(*This memory stops him in his tracks. He groans aloud; then he speaks in a low, furious voice.*)

NOSTROMO: I have been betrayed.

(*He waits a moment, backed up against a tree: then he grits his teeth and sets off again, into the darkness.*)

EXT. CUSTOMS HOUSE. NIGHT

NOSTROMO*'s still moving fast, and more stealthily, as he approaches the harbour. Tonight, there's a thin sliver of crescent moon in the starry sky.* NOSTROMO *stops dead; something has caught his eye.*

NOSTROMO*'s* POV*: up on the seaward corner of the looming building, a single light still burns in the room which was* SOTILLO*'s quarters.*

NOSTROMO *stares up at the lighted window for a moment, intrigued. Then he begins moving swiftly towards the building, resolved to investigate.*

INT. CUSTOMS HOUSE. NIGHT

NOSTROMO *squeezes through the massive doors and stops, immediately aware that something strange has occurred.*

His POV*: the great hall is full of acrid smoke and is dramatically illuminated by the shaft of light from the upstairs room. Suddenly, there's the sound of a shutter, slamming against a wall, somewhere upstairs.*

NOSTROMO *starts, as the sound echoes around the cavernous hall. He begins to move cautiously towards the staircase.* SOTILLO*'s troops have set a fire at the foot of the staircase, which has failed to ignite the hard wood and has burned down to a few smouldering embers, pinpoints of red light on the blackened bottom two steps.* NOSTROMO *hesitates at the foot of the stairs and looks up towards the light-source, its beams foggy in the drifting smoke.*

NOSTROMO *comes to a decision and springs as quickly and as lightly as he can up the staircase, protecting his bare feet against the smouldering wood.*

INT. LANDING. NIGHT

Half-way along the landing, NOSTROMO *suddenly stops and melts into a dark angle of the wall, where only the whites of his eyes are showing. He waits there a moment, then moves on.*

TRACKING SHOT, *his* POV*: the half-open door of* SOTILLO*'s room suddenly reveals something which causes* NOSTROMO *to freeze in his tracks: the shadow of a man, shapeless and high-shouldered, standing upright and motionless, with lowered head.*

NOSTROMO *hesitates. A piece of paper blown by a draught comes floating and scratching along the landing.* NOSTROMO, *slightly unnerved, looks back at the shadow, which hasn't moved. He decides on a tactical retreat.*

INT. CUSTOMS HOUSE. NIGHT

NOSTROMO *flits lightly down the stairs and heads for the door; still puzzled, he looks back up over his shoulder at the room upstairs and then runs smack into a man who's just entered the hallway. It's* DR MONYGHAM. *Both men let out a stifled exclamation; but of the two, it's* MONYGHAM *who seems the more surprised.*

MONYGHAM: You!

(NOSTROMO *raises a hand to his lips and whispers.*)

NOSTROMO: There's someone up there.

MONYGHAM: Sotillo. I've come to see him.

(*The extraordinariness of* NOSTROMO*'s presence seems to dawn on* MONYGHAM. *His voice also drops to a whisper.*)

What are you doing here? What's happened to the lighter?

NOSTROMO: Sunk. There was a collision.

(MONYGHAM *frowns, trying to make sense of this. Then he looks up the stairs again, focusing on the light from* SOTILLO*'s quarters.*)

MONYGHAM: Wait here.

NOSTROMO: I'm going.

MONYGHAM: Just wait for me a moment.

(NOSTROMO *watches, his expression still clouded with bitterness and doubt, as* MONYGHAM *hobbles up the stairs.*)

INT. LANDING. NIGHT

NOSTROMO*'s* POV*:* MONYGHAM *arrives on the landing.*

INT. CUSTOMS HOUSE. NIGHT

NOSTROMO *takes a step closer to the main door, ready to run.*

INT. LANDING. NIGHT

TRACKING SHOT*: following* MONYGHAM *as he limps briskly along the landing and pushes open the door to* SOTILLO*'s quarters.*

INT. SOTILLO'S QUARTERS. NIGHT

MONYGHAM *stops dead on the threshold, his mouth dropping open in shock.*

MONYGHAM*'s* POV*: there's a man standing with his back to him, casting the giant shadow on the wall. A split second later, however, it becomes clear that the man is dangling from a rope tied around his wrists and strung over a beam to an iron staple in the wall. His shoulders have been dislocated and his clenched fists forced up higher than his shoulder blades.*

MONYGHAM *struggles to overcome his nausea and fight back a host of terrible memories. His eyes travel downwards.*

The man's feet are six inches off the ground. Only one foot is wearing a shoe. There's a pool of blood on the floor. MONYGHAM *makes a supreme effort to pull himself together and calls back over his shoulder.*

MONYGHAM: Nostromo!

INT. CUSTOMS HOUSE. NIGHT

HIGH ANGLE SHOT*: looking down on* NOSTROMO *as he hears* MONYGHAM*'s voice.*

MONYGHAM: (*Off-screen*) Come up! Come up and see!

(*Reluctantly,* NOSTROMO *begins to move away from the door.*)

INT. SOTILLO'S QUARTERS. NIGHT

MONYGHAM *is calm now, perched on the edge of the desk, looking thoughtfully up at the body. As* NOSTROMO *appears in the doorway and stops, shaken by what he sees,* MONYGHAM *turns to him, gesturing in the direction of the body.*

MONYGHAM: Tortured; and then shot dead. Why, I wonder?

NOSTROMO: Who is it?
MONYGHAM: I don't know.

(NOSTROMO *looks up at the body. The room is lit by two short candles in iron candlesticks. He picks up one of them and begins to circle the body, holding the candle up to light the corpse's face.*

It's HIRSCH. *In his shock,* NOSTROMO *gasps and drops the candlestick, which clatters to the floor, extinguishing the candle. The softer light throws into relief the stars filling the window-frames. Silence, except for the lapping of the sea.*)

NOSTROMO: Hirsch. It's Hirsch. He was on the lighter.
MONYGHAM: How did he get here?
NOSTROMO: They must have picked him up. (*He looks up at the dark shape of the body and speaks with a kind of wounded tenderness.*) How could they torment him like this? He was such a coward: if they had shaken their fists at him he would have told them everything he knew.
MONYGHAM: Perhaps they didn't believe what he told them. (*He reflects for a moment.*) Yes: if he told Sotillo the lighter was sunk and the silver lost, how could Sotillo bear to believe him?

(NOSTROMO *looks at him, thoughtful, his eyes glittering in the darkness.*)

No, the real mystery is: why was he shot?

(*As they stand, looking up, there comes, on sound, a terrible wrenching thump, sigh of rope over wood, ripping of tendons.*)

INT. SOTILLO'S QUARTERS. DAY

An unidentifiable image fills the screen: mostly black, with dark red undulating masses and sharp yellowish edges. The image is accompanied by an unearthly sound: a dreadful howl of anguish, agonisingly protracted.

The camera draws back from the inside of HIRSCH*'s gaping mouth, as he continues to whimper and cry. Surprisingly, for the moment, he's alone in the room, hanging by his wrists from the estrapade. Above and behind him, high on the wall, the reflection of the sun on the sea, refracted through the jalousies, makes a beautiful sinuous rippling pattern.*

After a while, the homicidal MAJOR *steps into the room, followed by* SOTILLO. *The* MAJOR *gestures in* HIRSCH*'s direction, then sinks* *into a chair and watches as* SOTILLO *moves round* HIRSCH, *who stops whimpering when his eye falls on* SOTILLO *and directs towards him a desperate mute appeal.*

SOTILLO: Now: are you ready to tell me the truth?

HIRSCH: I have told you the truth. You ran the boat down. It sank. It must have.

SOTILLO: You expect me to believe that?

HIRSCH: But it's true!

(HIRSCH*'s fear and frustration erupt in a grating, whining wail, which has the effect of infuriating* SOTILLO. *He picks up his riding whip from the table and looks at* HIRSCH *again, threateningly. The* MAJOR *watches, moistening his lips in anticipation.*)

SOTILLO: The silver! Where have you hidden it?

(*In a frenzy now,* SOTILLO *launches himself at* HIRSCH, *lashing out with his whip, until the rope begins to twist and vibrate. Finally,* HIRSCH *cries out in agony.*)

HIRSCH: Nowhere!

(SOTILLO *looks up at him, now in a cold rage.*)

SOTILLO: You lying Jew.

(*All traces of pain and fear suddenly leave* HIRSCH*'s face. By a superhuman effort, he raises his head and gestures for* SOTILLO *to approach.* SOTILLO *moves towards him, waiting for his answer. Suddenly it comes, in the form of a great arc of spittle, projected into* SOTILLO*'s face with maximum force and accuracy.* SOTILLO *drops his whip and springs back, crying out in astonishment. Then, in a reflex action, he grabs his revolver from the desk and fires twice, at point-blank range, into* HIRSCH*'s heart.*

The MAJOR *springs to his feet in alarm.*)

MAJOR: What did you do that for?

(SOTILLO *looks completely panicked for a moment: then he wipes his face with his sleeve and attempts to affect a brazen nonchalance.*)

SOTILLO: I know exactly what I'm doing.

(*But the* MAJOR *continues to stare at him sceptically, unconvinced.*)

INT. SOTILLO'S QUARTERS. NIGHT

A match is struck. DR MONYGHAM *is relighting the candle dropped by* NOSTROMO.

MONYGHAM: Why shot?

(*The lighted candle reveals the anger in* NOSTROMO*'s face, as he looks up at* HIRSCH.)

NOSTROMO: What does it matter? (*His fraying patience suddenly seems to snap and he turns away.*) Out of my way.

(*He shoulders past* MONYGHAM *and hurries out of the room.* MONYGHAM *follows him as quickly as he can manage.*)

INT. LANDING. NIGHT

MONYGHAM *scuttles after* NOSTROMO, *grabs hold of his arm and succeeds in restraining him for a moment.*

MONYGHAM: Where are you going?

NOSTROMO: Back into town.

MONYGHAM: No, you mustn't. If you're seen you'll be arrested. Listen to me, I have a plan.

NOSTROMO: Always another plan. And I suppose this one also requires me to risk my life.

MONYGHAM: Yes.

(NOSTROMO *shakes free and moves away, hurrying down the stairs.*)

And me to risk mine.

INT. CUSTOMS HOUSE. NIGHT

NOSTROMO *slows on the stairs, intrigued in spite of himself.* MONYGHAM *moves down the stairs towards him.*

MONYGHAM: I shall distract Sotillo. I'll tell him I can help him find the silver.

NOSTROMO: Then you can look forward to a speedy death.

MONYGHAM: Maybe.

NOSTROMO: Or perhaps not so speedy. Perhaps slow enough to give me away.

(MONYGHAM *stops on the staircase, stricken.* NOSTROMO *has reached the bottom now and is moving towards the main doors.*)

MONYGHAM: Why did you say that?

(*He sets off again, hurrying crabwise down the stairs, moving too fast so that two steps from the bottom, he loses his footing and pitches face forward on to the earthen floor.* NOSTROMO *reluctantly returns to help him up; he's still extremely upset.*)

MONYGHAM: What have you heard?

NOSTROMO: Nothing.

MONYGHAM: If that's what you believe, why don't you kill me here and now?

(NOSTROMO *doesn't answer;* MONYGHAM *pulls himself together and dusts himself down.*)

I'm not going to betray you. And for a very simple reason. I need you.

NOSTROMO: What for?

(*His voice is dark with suspicion and reluctance.*)

MONYGHAM: Someone is needed to go to Cayta and bring back Barrios. I can arrange for a locomotive to be put at your disposal; that will take you to the railhead at the foot of the mountains. You could be back with him in ten days.

NOSTROMO: You think you could hold off Sotillo for that long?

MONYGHAM: When I can delay an answer no longer, I intend to tell him the silver is buried on the island of Great Isabel.

(NOSTROMO *gapes at him, aghast.*)

NOSTROMO: Three men could search that whole island in half a day. Then there would be nothing for Sotillo to do but cut your throat.

MONYGHAM: You have a better suggestion?

NOSTROMO: Tell him it's sunk.

MONYGHAM: You can hardly expect him to believe the truth. That was Hirsch's mistake.

NOSTROMO: No, I mean, tell him it's been hidden somewhere on the sea-bed, say in a line between the jetty and the breakwater. Then let him fish for it.

(MONYGHAM *ponders for a moment.*)

MONYGHAM: Yes. The very thing. You're a genius in your way, Nostromo.

NOSTROMO: It'll drive him mad. He'll see it every time he closes his eyes. There's something in a treasure that fastens on a man's mind.

(*He turns and slips out of the enormous door to the Customs House.*)

EXT. CUSTOMS HOUSE. NIGHT

MONYGHAM *has some difficulty catching up with* NOSTROMO.

MONYGHAM: You will bring back Barrios?

NOSTROMO: Why should I?

(MONYGHAM *chooses his words carefully.*)

MONYGHAM: Because if you succeed, your name will be famous from one end of America to the other.

NOSTROMO: I don't give a damn about your politics or your mines.

MONYGHAM: There are innocent people involved, whose little finger is worth more than you or me or Gould or the whole gang of them put together.

(*He's spoken with such intensity that* NOSTROMO, *mysteriously impressed, has stopped walking.* MONYGHAM *senses this may be the moment to press his advantage.*)

Go and wait at Viola's inn.

(*Suddenly,* NOSTROMO *grabs* MONYGHAM *roughly by the shoulders.*)

NOSTROMO: You don't care what may happen to me. Do you?

MONYGHAM: No more than I care what may happen to myself.

(NOSTROMO *finally speaks, his voice thick with anger.*)

NOSTROMO: If I do it, it won't be for you or for Don Carlos or for the good of the country: it'll be to avenge that poor miserable Hirsch.

INT. LIVING-ROOM IN THE ALBERGO D'ITALIA UNA. NIGHT

LINDA VIOLA *serves* NOSTROMO *with a hunk of bread and half an onion, into which he greedily sinks his teeth; meanwhile* GISELLE *is pouring him some red wine. Sitting against the wall, beneath the portrait of Garibaldi, looking stunned and helpless, is* VIOLA, *who speaks in Italian.*

VIOLA: You know what she said, Gian' Battista, the very last words she spoke?

(NOSTROMO *shakes his head, his mouth full.*)

She cried out: 'The children, Gian' Battista, save the children!'

(NOSTROMO *stops chewing, affected by this image.* LINDA *is watching him, her eyes bright.*)

And before I could take her hands, she was dead. And without a priest.

(Into the ensuing silence, comes the hiss and clatter of an approaching railway engine. NOSTROMO, *not without relief, springs to his feet, drains the wine and pushes the bread and onion inside his shirt.*

LINDA *catches hold of his arm, her expression fierce. She speaks in English.)*

LINDA: You mustn't leave us again, Gian' Battista.

NOSTROMO: I have to do this, Linda.

LINDA: Why? Why do you put yourself in this terrible danger? She begged you not to.

(As NOSTROMO *struggles to free himself from her grip,* GISELLE *suddenly speaks with a surprising quiet authority.)*

GISELLE: Let him go.

(LINDA *shoots a furious glance at her sister, but in her surprise she's released* NOSTROMO, *who hurries to the door.* VIOLA *watches him, rooted to his chair;* LINDA *and* GISELLE *follow him.)*

EXT. ALBERGO. NIGHT

An engine bears down the track under a great head of steam, lit by the red glow from its furnace, slowing as its whistle lets out a low hiss.

NOSTROMO *stops to kiss the girls,* LINDA *first and then* GISELLE, *the latter with discernibly more enthusiasm. Her eyes are shining with hero-worship.*

The engine slows. The driver, a black, bare-chested giant, helps MONYGHAM *down from the footplate. He stumbles, only just keeping his balance. Meanwhile, timing it perfectly,* NOSTROMO *sprints up the embankment and leaps gracefully on to the footplate.*

The GIRLS *watch, spellbound as* NOSTROMO *vanishes into the cab, the engine emits a great cloud of steam and begins to gather speed.*

Great tears roll down LINDA*'s cheeks. She puts an arm round* GISELLE *and draws her close as, in the distance, there's the sound of gunfire.* MONYGHAM *stands at the top of the embankment, watching the train disappear, exhilarated, as the train whistle blows, a long, triumphant blast.*

EXT. OUTSKIRTS OF SULACO. NIGHT

The engine is surrounded by a platoon of MONTERO*'s soldiers on horseback, keeping pace, firing their rifles.*

INT. ENGINE. NIGHT

Bullets smack and whine against the steel plates of the engine. The driver, calmly shovelling on coal, indicates to NOSTROMO *a kind of rucksack in the corner, with the handle of a revolver sticking out of it, and* NOSTROMO *reaches for the revolver.*

EXT. ENGINE. NIGHT

NOSTROMO *leans out on the footplate, takes aim and fires. For the moment, he hasn't seen, looming up in front of the engine, the wooden barricade built to block the track. He becomes aware of it just in time to dive back into the engine.*

EXT. OUTSKIRTS OF SULACO. NIGHT

In a shower of sparks, the engine smashes through the barricade, carrying debris away in front of it down the tracks.

UNDERWATER. DAY

A pale hand moves carefully over the ocean floor, exploring. There are ten or a dozen divers, fanned out, searching the sea-bed. Their breath is beginning to run out and one by one they peel off, heading towards the surface.

EXT. DECK OF THE STEAMER. DAY

SOTILLO *is leaning over the side of the steamer he commandeered, watching as, below, the divers begin to surface. As they all indicate their empty-handedness,* SOTILLO *turns exasperatedly to* MONYGHAM, *who sits nearby on the deck.* MONYGHAM *shrugs and* SOTILLO *turns back to shout down over the side.*

SOTILLO: Go down again!

(*Not far off, the* MAJOR *is watching* SOTILLO, *his expression contemptuous.*

SOTILLO *turns to* MONYGHAM, *his expression black.*)

Well, Doctor, I'm not sure how much longer I can be responsible for your safety.

(MONYGHAM *stands, calm and motionless; he turns his head, looking out south across the Gulf.*)

EXT. ENTRADA PASS. DAY

LONG SHOT: *a tiny figure, on horseback, rounds one of the highest snow-capped peaks of the Cordillera.*

CLOSE *on* NOSTROMO *as he reins in his horse. He's wrapped in blankets against the cold and his breath rises in the air.*

EXT. HINTERLAND. DAY

NOSTROMO*'s* POV*: far below are the deserts and plains of Costaguana, awe-inspiring, washed in bright sunlight, stretching away as far as the eye can see.*

EXT. ENTRADA PASS. DAY

CLOSE *on* NOSTROMO*: he looks grimly determined. He makes a sound, urging his mare forward.*

EXT. ISLAND OF GREAT ISABEL. DAY

It's towards evening and DECOUD *stands by the dinghy in the ravine looking down at an open metal box which contains dried meat and hard tack. He stares at the food for a moment, fingering it listlessly, then closes the box and drops it back into the dinghy. He moves away down towards the sea, staring up into the air as he goes, looking for something. Eventually, he comes to a ragged halt, lowers his head and shakes it, muttering to himself.*

DECOUD: Not even a bird.

(*He trudges on, round the point and comes to a halt again. Below, on the sand, is the half-rotted carcase of a dolphin. For a long moment,* DECOUD *stands looking down at the remains, his expression grief-stricken.*)

EXT. ENTRANCE TO THE MINE. DAY

Thick fuse wire unspools jerkily from a wooden winch. The camera pans upwards into the black mouth of the mine.

INT. TUNNEL IN THE MINE. DAY

DON PEPE *holds up an oil-lamp and watches* GOULD *as he carefully installs a bundle of dynamite in a recess in the rock. They move on, unwinding more wire as they go.*

EXT. THE PARAMO DE IVIE. NIGHT
The wind howls across the bare rocky plateau, enveloping NOSTROMO *and his horse in fine snow whipped off the surface of the glacier. They're making slow progress down the steep slope.*

EXT. ISLAND OF GREAT ISABEL. NIGHT
Although the shelter of the tree is not far away, DECOUD *stands, grimy and unshaven, in the pouring rain. It's not clear if it's raindrops or tears rolling down his cheeks. After a while, he throws back his head and cries out:*
DECOUD: Antonia!

INT. MRS GOULD'S BEDROOM. NIGHT
MRS GOULD *wakes with a start: behind the sound of the pouring rain is another, grimmer rumble: the thunder of horses' hooves.*

INT. GRAN SALA. NIGHT
MRS GOULD *runs barefoot across the room.*

EXT. BALCONY. NIGHT
MRS GOULD *steps out on to the balcony.*

EXT. CALLE DE LA CONSTITUCIÓN. NIGHT
Below, MONTERO, *resplendent in a new uniform, the rain dripping off the tip of his Aztec nose, rides at the head of a mounted column of troops, heading off towards the mountains.*

EXT. BALCONY. NIGHT
This is what MRS GOULD *has been afraid of: she raises her eyes and looks in the direction of the San Tomé gorge, her expression full of fear.*

EXT. SALT FLATS. DAY
A shimmering miasma of heat-haze and fine white dust from which two stumbling figures gradually emerge: NOSTROMO *and his horse, which he's leading across a vast moonscape of salt. He pulls up his bandanna to protect his nose and mouth and then staggers on, a ghostly spectre.*

EXT. ISLAND OF GREAT ISABEL. DAY

The highest point of the island, on the cliff above the ravine.

DECOUD *is jumping up and down, frantically waving his frock-coat above his head, shouting incoherently across the silence of the Gulf.*

DECOUD: Help! Help!

EXT. OCEAN. DAY

DECOUD*'s* POV*: a distant sail moves inexorably away, towards the horizon.*

EXT. LOWER WORKINGS OF THE MINE. DAY

MONTERO *raises a hand to halt his column. Then he looks around him, puzzled.*

The village and mine workings are completely deserted and silent except for the sounds of the surrounding jungle and the screech of the birds. The flimsy front door of a cottage has been left open and swings to and fro squeaking on its hinges in the breeze.

MONTERO*'s horse whinnies nervously and other horses in the column show signs of restlessness. Then, as the surrounding jungle sounds noticeably die away,* MONTERO*'s horse rears, showing the whites of its eyes.*

Suddenly, from above, comes a strange distant rumbling sound, which gradually increases in volume like an approaching earthquake. As MONTERO *looks up, frowning, the tranquillity of the scene is violently shattered as ton upon ton of rock and rubble and silver ore comes crashing off the modified chutes on to* MONTERO*'s army.*

EXT. ENTRANCE TO THE MINE. DAY

At the top of the chutes stands GOULD*, his arms folded, his expression grimly satisfied.*

EXT. LOWER WORKINGS OF THE MINE. DAY

Chaotic images of dust and panic, terrified horses and crushed soldiers.

MONTERO*, coated with dust, looks about him in a state of shock. When the rumble from above starts up again, he doesn't hesitate. Like the rest of his troops who are still intact, he spurs his horse to gallop away from the danger zone, back the way he came.*

EXT. DESERT. DAY

LONG SHOT: NOSTROMO, *on horseback, moves away from the camera through the bizarre and twisted shapes of giant cacti, standing like deformed sentinels in a weird landscape.*

CLOSE *on a machete blade as it decapitates a cactus.* NOSTROMO *dismounts, dips his hands into the cache of water contained within the cactus and drinks, gulping greedily.*

EXT. ISLAND OF GREAT ISABEL. DAY

DECOUD *stands knee-deep in the sea, staring hopelessly across at the mainland, a couple of miles away. A thought suddenly strikes him and he reaches in his inside pocket to find the draft of the Declaration of Independence he wrote in the Albergo d'Italia Una. He utters a mirthless, brief laugh and begins strewing the document, page by page, across the surface of the sea.*

DECOUD: We hold these truths to be self-evident . . .

EXT. BEACH IN CAYTA. NIGHT

A horse's hooves, wrapped in sacking, move to the end of a cobbled street, on to a sandy beach and down to the water's edge.

NOSTROMO *dismounts and removes the sacking, looking down the beach where a picket fence extends to the sea and camp-fires burn; and beyond, the lights of a fort, his objective.*

He remounts and, silhouetted against the moonlit sea, speeds from a walk to a canter. Finally, crouched down in the saddle, he's galloping full tilt through the shallow water, past the fence and the guards, who open fire at him far too late.

EXT. OCEAN. DAY

The prow of a coaster cuts through the grey ocean.

EXT. BRIDGE OF THE COASTER. DAY

NOSTROMO *and* BARRIOS *stand, side by side, on the bridge. Behind them, smoke billows out of the funnel. Below, the decks are jammed with* BARRIOS*'s troops.*

EXT. RAVINE ON GREAT ISABEL. DAWN

DECOUD *looks appalling: a week's growth of beard, his clothes filthy and tattered. He's on his hands and knees, scrabbling at the sand where the silver is buried. He's made a big enough hole to expose the silver; and now he begins to wrench out the loose bars. It's light but the sun is not yet up.*

INT. MONYGHAM'S CABIN. DAWN

The cabin door bursts open and SOTILLO *appears in the doorway. He looks demented. He's accompanied by two guards and a short, overweight priest with a prayer-book.* MONYGHAM *seems calmer than he is.*

SOTILLO: I've brought you a priest.

MONYGHAM: No, that won't be necessary.

(SOTILLO *shrugs and motions the priest to stand aside.*)

EXT. BANKS OF THE STREAM ON GREAT ISABEL. DAY

The open lid of a biscuit tin provides a distorted reflection of DECOUD, *who has finished shaving with a cut-throat razor; he puts down tin and razor, rinses his face in the stream, and, using the biscuit tin again, makes a final adjustment to his fashionably-knotted cravat.*

EXT. BEACH. DAY

DECOUD *lowers four ingots of silver gently into the bottom of the little dinghy. Then he pushes it out to sea and scrambles aboard.*

EXT. DINGHY. DAWN

The dinghy is out in the Gulf now. DECOUD *ships his oars, leans forward, picks up the ingots and puts two in each side-pocket of his frock-coat. Then he relaxes, motionless on the thwart, his head up, his expression serene. He's waiting.*

EXT. GOLFO PLACIDO. DAWN

The sun comes up, glorious over the mountain range.

LONG SHOT, *with the dinghy at its centre, as the Gulf erupts into a vast sheet of glittering gold.*

EXT. DECK OF THE STEAMER. DAY

A rope snakes over the yard-arm and falls back to the deck. Drums. Solemn atmosphere. SOTILLO*'s troops line the deck. The* MAJOR *lowers a noose over* MONYGHAM*'s head.* SOTILLO *watches, his eyes stuck out like billiard balls.*

MONYGHAM *is afraid, but he's succeeded in composing his features into an expression of stoical contempt.*

Suddenly, there's a strange whistling sound. SOTILLO *frowns and then panics completely as a shell explodes amidships. Pandemonium ensues.*

MONYGHAM *stands motionless, his hands tied behind his back. He turns his head, looking out across the Gulf.*

EXT. GOLFO PLACIDO. DAY

MONYGHAM*'s* POV*:* BARRIOS*'s coaster bears down on the steamer. It fires another shell.*

EXT. SAN TOMÉ GORGE. DAY

Standing on the lip of the gorge, his hand shading his eyes, GOULD *stares down across the plain.*

His POV*: far below, in the Gulf, the size of a child's toy,* BARRIOS*'s coaster closes on the steamer, emitting tiny puffs of smoke, which, after some delay, translate themselves into the dull thumps of a naval barrage.*

GOULD *watches, extremely pleased.*

EXT. DECK OF THE STEAMER. DAY

The coaster has drawn up alongside the steamer and NOSTROMO *leads a boarding-party, jumping down on to the slightly lower main deck of the steamer.* NOSTROMO *is unarmed, but* BARRIOS*'s troops wield the impressive repeaters brought over by* DECOUD.

SOTILLO*'s men are surrendering as promptly as possible.* NOSTROMO *strides down the deck, avoiding the smouldering craters and corpses, on his way towards* MONYGHAM*, still tied up on the poop-deck.*

MONYGHAM*'s* POV *as* NOSTROMO *arrives and unties him. Before he can speak, he sees something and indicates it to* NOSTROMO*, who turns.*

NOSTROMO*'s* POV*:* SOTILLO *approaches from the wheel-house, waving a white silk handkerchief.*

NOSTROMO *frowns and then begins moving purposefully towards* SOTILLO.

SOTILLO *hesitates and falters to a stop.*

SOTILLO*'s* POV*:* NOSTROMO *is bearing down on him with an expression of cold ferocity.*

SOTILLO *drops his handkerchief and begins fumbling desperately in his pocket.*

NOSTROMO*'s* POV*: the sight of* SOTILLO*'s revolver doesn't deter him in the slightest and he's almost on top of him by the time it goes off. Miraculously, in* SOTILLO*'s panic, the bullet has gone wide and now* NOSTROMO *takes his arm in a vice-like grip and twists until* SOTILLO *is obliged to drop the gun.* NOSTROMO *releases his arm.* SOTILLO *looks wildly at* NOSTROMO, *then down at the revolver. He makes a desperate lunge for it, but* NOSTROMO *grabs him, throws a burly forearm round his neck and squeezes. There's a crack like a pistol-shot, as* SOTILLO*'s neck is broken.* MONYGHAM*'s eyes widen as he watches* NOSTROMO *pick up* SOTILLO*'s body and drop it over the side.*

NOSTROMO *remains standing at the rail. He's seen something out to sea.*

EXT. GOLFO PLACIDO. DAY

NOSTROMO*'s* POV*:* DECOUD*'s dinghy, floating, empty now, on the calm waters.*

EXT. DECK OF THE STEAMER. DAY

NOSTROMO *comes to an abrupt decision and starts pulling off his boots.*

MONYGHAM *watches, as* NOSTROMO *scrambles up on to the rail and executes a perfect dive down into the sea: he's fascinated, but extremely puzzled.*

EXT. GOLFO PLACIDO. DAY

NOSTROMO *reaches up and hauls himself aboard the dinghy.*

EXT. DINGHY. DAY

Almost immediately, NOSTROMO *notices the bloodstain on the gunwale. He drops to one knee to investigate, running his finger over the stain. Finally he sits back against the thwart, pondering.*

The sound of a shot, followed by a splash.

UNDERWATER. DAY

DECOUD*'s body sinks fast through the blue, a skein of blood rising.*

His revolver lands on the ocean floor, releasing a puff of sand.

EXT. DINGHY. DAY

Having interpreted the facts to his own satisfaction, NOSTROMO *takes up the oars, still profoundly pensive.*

EXT. BEACH ON GREAT ISABEL. DAY

NOSTROMO *grounds the dinghy, jumps out and hauls it up on to the beach.*

EXT. RAVINE ON GREAT ISABEL. DAY

NOSTROMO *runs into the ravine and immediately sees the hole dug by* DECOUD *and the dull glint of silver. He hurries over to it and drops to his knees. He reaches in and pulls out an ingot. He's entirely bemused. He goes over to the tree, the ingot in his hand and sits, leaning against it, lost in thought. Automatically, he begins wiping smudges of earth from the silver.*

UNDERWATER. DAY

DECOUD *sits on the ocean floor, his revolver not far off, his mouth set in a sinister rictus.*

EXT. BEACH ON GREAT ISABEL. DAY

It's much later in the day. NOSTROMO *stands on the beach. Part of the town is on fire: there's a red glow and huge billowing clouds of black smoke. The sound of distant gunfire travels across the water.*

NOSTROMO*'s face. He's watching but he seems hardly to be registering what's happening. Suddenly, there's an enormous explosion nearby and* NOSTROMO *starts and looks to his right.*

EXT. GOLFO PLACIDO. DAY

NOSTROMO*'s* POV*: the fluttering Stars and Stripes, astern of the USS* Powhatan, *seen as the cruiser slides past the island, making full speed for the harbour.*

EXT. COASTAL PLAIN. DAY

GOULD *pauses at the head of his column of miners, mostly Indians mounted on a motley assortment of mules, donkeys and pit-ponies, wearing the green-and-white company ponchos and armed with knives, axes and sledge-hammers.*

EXT. GOLFO PLACIDO. DAY

GOULD'*s* POV*: below, as before, the ships manœuvre like toys, as the* Powhatan *fires another thunderous salvo from its big eight-inch guns, causing numerous explosions in the town.*

He spurs on his horse, his eyes shining with exhilaration.

EXT. BEACH ON GREAT ISABEL. DAY

The sun is low in the sky and the sharp-etched Cordillera towers above the battle-scarred port of Sulaco. NOSTROMO *shakes his head, somewhere between indifference and exasperation, and turns his back on the distant clash of ignorant armies.*

EXT. RAVINE ON GREAT ISABEL. DAY

NOSTROMO *sits, resting against the tree again. He reaches for the ingot, lifts it to him, dusts it off, weighs it in his hand.*

CLOSE *on the bar of silver: it fills the screen.*

CLOSE *on* NOSTROMO*: he looks up and speaks very quietly.*

NOSTROMO: I must grow rich very slowly.

SLOW FADE TO BLACK

EXT. GOLFO PLACIDO. DAY

A beautiful schooner rounds a rocky point of the Great Isabel, gliding across a glassy sea.

A caption:

SIX YEARS LATER

EXT. SULACO. DAY

ANOTHER ANGLE *shows the harbour, the town and the mountain range.*

A caption:

THE PORT OF SULACO
IN THE REPUBLIC OF SULACO
1900

EXT. SCHOONER. DAY

NOSTROMO, *glowing with health and prosperity, stands on deck, looking to landward. All of a sudden, his eyes register profound shock and dismay.*

EXT. ISLAND OF GREAT ISABEL. DAY

NOSTROMO'*s* POV*: on top of the cliff, above the ravine where the silver is buried, is a half-built lighthouse, surrounded by scaffolding. Workmen swarm over the site. A couple of them stop to wave to the schooner.*

EXT. SCHOONER. DAY

NOSTROMO *has the presence of mind to wave back. Then he raises his binoculars to his eyes.*

EXT. RAVINE. DAY

BINOCULAR SHOT*:* PAN *and the ravine comes into view. It's quite undisturbed.*

EXT. SCHOONER. DAY

NOSTROMO *lowers the binoculars, unmistakably relieved; then frowns as he notices something else and raises them again.*

EXT. GREAT ISABEL. DAY

BINOCULAR SHOT*: a small cottage is under construction on the slope between the lighthouse and the beach.*

EXT. CALLE DE LA CONSTITUCIÓN. DAY

NOSTROMO, *now in a good brown English suit and kid gloves, drives his elegant carriage past the repainted façade, down the resurfaced street.*

EXT. PLAZA MAYOR. DAY

The Plaza has been transformed: an elaborate new fountain plays in the centre; the Intendencia has been handsomely refurbished and a bell-tower is under construction on top of it; the gardens of the Alameda are lush and well-tended; there's a small orchestra playing 'Tales From the Vienna Woods' on the bandstand and an open-air café with gingham tablecloths. A tram clatters across the square; and NOSTROMO'*s carriage pulls up outside the Amarilla Club next to a primitive automobile. With the new century, prosperity has come to Sulaco.*

EXT. AMARILLA CLUB. DAY

The mossy statue of the bishop in the little patio outside the Club has been replaced with a new bronze statue of a man holding papers and a quill pen. A woman in black is arranging flowers in front of the statue; she half-turns as NOSTROMO *passes and he inclines his head respectfully: it's* ANTONIA AVELLANOS.

NOSTROMO: Donna Antonia.

ANTONIA: Captain Fidanza.

(*He passes on into the Club and she returns to her work: at which point the plaque beneath the statue becomes visible. It reads: Don Martin Decoud (1860–1894)* MAN OF LETTERS. PATRIOT, FOUNDING FATHER OF THE REPUBLIC OF SULACO.)

INT. AMARILLA CLUB. DAY

The former billiard-room has been transformed into a very well-appointed dining-room, in which NOSTROMO *is lunching with* CHARLES GOULD, *who is ageing well and looks lean and fit, although his features are somewhat drawn. Behind him, almost covering one wall, is a monumental heroic painting, in which he features, although the central event described by the picture is the drawing of an enraged* GENERAL MONTERO *in a specially-constructed wooden cage across the plaza, taunted by a mounted* GENERAL BARRIOS.

GOULD: The port is so busy now, it seemed a necessary safeguard.

NOSTROMO: Well, of course: but the question I wanted to put to you is whether or not a lighthouse-keeper has been appointed?

GOULD: Not that I know of.

NOSTROMO: I happen to know old Giorgio Viola is thinking of selling the Albergo . . .

(GOULD *considers for a moment.*)

GOULD: Isn't he rather old to be taking on new responsibilities?

NOSTROMO: He has his daughters.

(GOULD *looks dubious.*)

I know you have shown me too many kindnesses already. When you gave me my schooner . . .

GOULD: We felt it was the least we could do. Without you we

would scarcely be sitting here today. And in any case, you insisted on paying us back within three years.

NOSTROMO: I don't like to feel beholden. And business has been good.

GOULD: Evidently. Well. I'll see what I can do.

NOSTROMO: Thank you.

GOULD: You just caught me. I have business in Europe and America and I leave at the end of the week. Mrs Gould and I will be away for some months.

NOSTROMO: I never think of Europe.

(GOULD *doesn't quite know how to respond to this straightforward remark, with its hint of melancholy: he falls back on his customary businesslike air.*)

GOULD: I'll get on to this today.

(NOSTROMO *smiles, in grateful acknowledgement. They eat on in silence.*)

FADE

FADE IN

EXT. LIGHTHOUSE. DAY

The lighthouse is completed: a white tower on top of the cliff.

INT. LAMP ROOM IN THE LIGHTHOUSE. DAY

An extravaganza of glass: outside, the lozenge-shaped panes reveal an infinity of sky and sea; inside, the revolving mechanism which surrounds the lamp, constructed out of magnifying glass and blacked-out panels, stationary at present, has a strange, distorting effect on those parts of the confined space which are seen through it. LINDA VIOLA *comes clattering up the wooden stairs, leading* NOSTROMO *by the hand. Bringing up the rear, dragging her feet somewhat, is* GISELLE.

LINDA: Here . . .

(NOSTROMO *leans forward, examining the optics.* LINDA *watches him, her eyes bright.*)

I trim the wicks and check the level of the oil. (*She pushes a lever and the mechanism surrounding the lamp purrs into life and begins to revolve.*) And this carries the beam, all the way out across the Gulf.

(NOSTROMO, *from her* POV*: he bends forward, magnified by the glass, fascinated by the workings of the mechanism. Then he looks up and sees:*

LINDA, *also magnified, looking at him, her eyes glittering with intensity: until a blacked-out panel passes in front of her and she disappears.*

NOSTROMO *straightens up and glances at* GISELLE, *to find she's also looking at him. She turns away to stare indifferently out across the Gulf.*)

If you paid attention, you might learn something.

GISELLE: I've told you before, I don't understand machines. (*She turns back to* NOSTROMO.) Gian' Battista, why did you have us banished to this island?

LINDA: You know the Albergo was far too much for Father. Don't be so ungrateful.

GISELLE: I'm not ungrateful. Really I'm not.

(*She fixes* NOSTROMO *with a bold stare. A slightly uncomfortable silence is broken by the sound of old* VIOLA*'s* VOICE *calling 'Linda . . .'.* LINDA *switches off the mechanism and hurries to answer the summons. The sound of her feet, clattering down the stairs.*

NOSTROMO*'s* POV*: the mechanism comes to a halt so that* GISELLE *is seen through the glass, magnified.*

She looks exquisite.

CLOSE *on* NOSTROMO*: he's riveted.*

His POV*: suddenly* GISELLE*'s image vanishes and the real* GISELLE *appears magically beside him, smiling enigmatically.*)

I like to dance.

(*They look at each other for a moment, both with expressions of open desire. Then* NOSTROMO *crosses to the door where he hesitates and turns to allow* GISELLE *to go first. The doorway's so narrow, she's obliged to press past him, blushing. He stays where he is for a moment, closing his eyes, shaken by disturbing thoughts.*)

EXT. CALLE DE LA CONSTITUCIÓN. DAY

A shiny automobile putters down the road: it's driven by CHARLES GOULD. *Next to him, in a travelling veil, is* MRS GOULD. *Behind, their old landau follows, driven by* IGNACIO, *piled high with cabin trunks and monogrammed suitcases.*

EXT. PATIO IN THE CASA GOULD. DAY

A brilliant rectangle of light, as the small door opens in the great door. MRS GOULD *passes under the archway, pinning back her veil.*

Hurrying towards her, down a line of servants in their best livery, is a man transformed: DR MONYGHAM, *resplendent in frock-coat, wing-collar and bow tie. For a moment he seems about to kiss her but he restrains himself.*

MRS GOULD: Well, Dr Monygham, have you missed us?

MONYGHAM: I've . . . (*He breaks off as the great doors swing open and* GOULD *appears, sauntering under the archway; and adopts his customary persona.*) Not in the least, been far too busy.

GOULD: Doctor. (*They shake hands crisply.*) How is everything up at the mine?

MONYGHAM: Oh . . . flourishing.

(*They're bringing in the landau with the luggage; and* MONYGHAM *feels suddenly overcome.*)

I'll leave you to yourselves, you must be tired. I'll call tomorrow, if I may?

MRS GOULD: Yes, come to lunch, dear Dr Monygham. And come early.

GOULD: Don't expect to find me.

(MRS GOULD *looks up at him involuntarily, distressed.*)

I'll be off at dawn. To the mine.

(*He smiles coolly at his wife.*)

Give you a chance to catch up on all the gossip.

(MONYGHAM *nods, turns and starts to hobble away.*)

INT. MRS GOULD'S BEDROOM. NIGHT

MRS GOULD *is sitting at her dressing-table when* GOULD *appears in the doorway.*

MRS GOULD: Do you really have to go up there tomorrow?

GOULD: I'm very anxious to see that everything is in order.

MRS GOULD: And what about our life? Is everything in order there?

GOULD: I'm . . . not sure I know what you mean. (*He looks away for a moment.*) For some reason, when we were away, I kept thinking of my father. How I wish he could have known what would be built up from his inheritance.

MRS GOULD: I had plenty of time to think, as well, with you

away at all those meetings. I remembered all those plans we used to have.

GOULD: In the long run, it's often more productive to reinvest capital than to distribute it. We do what we can.

MRS GOULD: But I'd always hoped we might do what we wanted to. I didn't understand that material interests showed no mercy.

(GOULD *is silent: and now* MRS GOULD *rises and goes over to embrace him. He takes her, reluctantly, in his arms. Eventually, she looks up at him.*)

Stay.

GOULD: I have to get up very early. (*He leans down and gives her a perfunctory kiss.*) Goodnight, my dear.

(*He leaves the room, abruptly.* MRS GOULD*'s head sinks: then she looks up. Very faintly, through the window, comes the sound of the distant stamping-mills. A thought strikes her. She reaches out and picks up the original ingot of silver; she contemplates it for a moment, then bundles it away into one of the drawers of her bureau. Tears begin to sparkle in her eyes.*)

EXT. ISLAND OF GREAT ISABEL. DAY

The screen is filled with screeching seagulls. The source of their indignation is NOSTROMO, *who now climbs into frame, moving up the rocky slope which leads from the main beach to the lighthouse. It's late afternoon and he's wearing his white shirt and red sash. He's preoccupied and therefore startled when* GIORGIO VIOLA *steps out from behind a rock with a rifle in his hand. As soon as he sees it's* NOSTROMO *he puts the rifle up and embraces him. Dialogue in Italian.*

VIOLA: Gian' Battista!

NOSTROMO: What's the matter?

(*The old man murmurs to him conspiratorially.*)

VIOLA: There's a thief on this island.

(NOSTROMO *looks at him, momentarily shocked.*)

NOSTROMO: What do you mean?

VIOLA: I hear strange noises at night. Once I saw a boat in the moonlight, near that little beach.

(*He points down in the direction of the ravine.* NOSTROMO *laughs uneasily.*)

NOSTROMO: You must have dreamt it.

VIOLA: No, no. (*They walk on for a moment, in silence.*) The girls will be happy you're here.

NOSTROMO: Don't call them for a moment: there's something I want to discuss with you.

(VIOLA *looks up at him quickly and smiles, nodding his head knowledgeably.*)

VIOLA: Speak.

(*But* NOSTROMO *walks on in silence, his expression constrained.*)

EXT. VIOLA'S COTTAGE ON THE ISLAND. DAY

LONG SHOT: NOSTROMO *and* VIOLA *arrive outside* VIOLA*'s neat whitewashed cottage.* VIOLA *leans his rifle up against the wall and sits on a wooden bench. He looks up at* NOSTROMO, *amused.*

VIOLA: Speak.

(NOSTROMO *paces up and down for a moment. Then he goes and sits beside* VIOLA.)

NOSTROMO: We both know what Signora Teresa asked of me on the night she died.

(VIOLA*'s smile becomes even broader.*)

VIOLA: Yes.

NOSTROMO: But I also know how much you depend on Linda for the running of the lighthouse.

VIOLA: Not at all.

(*He springs to his feet, very happy.* NOSTROMO *tries hurriedly to correct the misunderstanding.*)

NOSTROMO: So instead, I have decided to ask you . . .

(*But* VIOLA *is not listening.*)

VIOLA: Linda!

NOSTROMO: No, I . . .

VIOLA: I understand what you're saying Gian' Battista and I'm touched: but nothing in the world would prevent me from honouring the soul of my beloved Teresa.

(CLOSE *on* LINDA, *as she appears in the doorway.*)

Here is your husband!

(*A rapturous expression lights up* LINDA*'s face: she runs across and buries herself in* NOSTROMO*'s arms, speaking to him in English.*)

LINDA: Since I was a child, Gian' Battista, I have lived only for you.

(*She reaches up, takes his face between her hands and kisses him passionately on the lips. They move apart,* LINDA *ecstatic,* NOSTROMO *with a haunted expression. His eyes widen as he sees:*

GISELLE, *standing in the doorway of the cottage, her fair hair burnished by the setting sun.*)

EXT. LIGHTHOUSE. EVENING

The lighthouse rears up, sharply silhouetted against the evening sky.

EXT. VIOLA'S COTTAGE. EVENING

VIOLA *empties a glass of red wine.* NOSTROMO *and* LINDA *are on the bench, her arms tightly clasped around him.* GISELLE *sits on her own, a little way off, embroidering an altar-cloth. Behind them, on the horizon, a red sun dips into a purple sea. Dialogue in Italian.*

VIOLA: Linda. The light, the light!

(LINDA *sits up, startled.*)

LINDA: Of course, Father, I'm sorry.

VIOLA: Don't forget your duty.

(*She scrambles up: and, impulsively, she rushes over to* GISELLE *and covers her face with kisses. Then she comes back to kiss* NOSTROMO *and hurries away in the direction of the lighthouse. Meanwhile,* VIOLA *has risen to his feet.*)

I'm going to cook the supper. (*He begins to move off, then turns back to* GISELLE *and adds:*) And you, little one, now we must start looking for a husband for you. God grant you find a man as good as this.

(*He disappears into the cottage. For a long moment, there's silence and no movement. Then,* GISELLE *looks up to find* NOSTROMO*'s eyes burning into her. They speak English to one another, their voices husky and staccato, the words tumbling over one another. Darkness has fallen.*)

NOSTROMO: Is there somebody?

GISELLE: There might be.

NOSTROMO: Who? Who is it?

(*He's spoken so sharply and moved across to her so quickly, that she looks up at him in alarm.*)

Do you love him?
GISELLE: No, of course not, I . . .
NOSTROMO: And does he love you?
GISELLE: He says he does, but . . .
NOSTROMO: Who is this?
(He breaks off as she looks up at him again, in supplication. Then, involuntarily, he speaks, almost in a whisper, as his hand reaches out to touch her hair.)
Your hair is like gold.
(She blushes in the half-light: then tries to adopt a bantering tone.)
GISELLE: Perhaps now Linda will stop being so fierce with me: now you've told her what she's been waiting so long to hear.
NOSTROMO: I've told her nothing. Do you know why?
GISELLE: Gian' Battista . . .
(Her protest is cut short as, suddenly, above them, the light pours out of the lighthouse tower. It begins to revolve and there's silence until the beam moves across GISELLE*'s face.* NOSTROMO *drops to one knee beside her.)*
NOSTROMO: I've told her nothing, because it's you that I love.
(The beam of light passes across GISELLE*'s face again: revealing that her shock is tempered by an unmistakable pleasure.)*
I came here this evening to ask for you, not your sister. Your father misunderstood me, he wouldn't listen.
GISELLE: Tell him again, make him listen!
NOSTROMO: I can't.
GISELLE: Why not?
NOSTROMO: If he knew I wanted you instead of Linda, he would banish me from the island. *(The beam passes again.* NOSTROMO *takes* GISELLE*'s hand.)* Come. Walk with me.
(She stands up. The altar-cloth falls from her lap to the ground. He leads her towards the deeper obscurity of the side-wall of the cottage. Their voices are scarcely audible, as if they hardly dared to speak.)
And you love me.
GISELLE: Of course.
(They've reached the corner of the cottage, where the lighthouse

beam cannot reach them. NOSTROMO *takes her face in his hands and begins kissing her greedily.*)

EXT. LIGHTHOUSE. NIGHT

The top half of the lighthouse: the beam stabs out into the night.

EXT. SIDE-WALL OF THE COTTAGE. NIGHT

NOSTROMO *pins* GISELLE *back against the white wall: their dark shapes writhe and entwine.*

EXT. LIGHTHOUSE. NIGHT

At an angle, looking up at the lamp-room: the beam comes scything round through the darkness.

EXT. SIDE-WALL OF THE COTTAGE. NIGHT

The extremest edge of the beam picks out NOSTROMO*'s hand, pinning* GISELLE*'s hand back against the wall.*

EXT. LIGHTHOUSE. NIGHT

On a level with the lamp-room: as the beam comes round, the screen explodes into dazzling light.

EXT. SIDE-WALL OF THE COTTAGE. NIGHT

NOSTROMO *and* GISELLE *are on the ground now: he's kissing her passionately. Her head arches back and she gasps aloud.*

INT. LAMP-ROOM. NIGHT

LINDA *moves restlessly about the room. The lamp's mechanism whirrs and clicks: as it revolves, bright splinters of light spill out from the edges of the prisms.*

LINDA *sits down and stares at the lamp, troubled. Pinpoints and refractions of light dance across her worried face.*

EXT. SIDE-WALL OF THE COTTAGE. NIGHT

CLOSE *on* GISELLE*'s face, streaked with tears in the moonlight. She's lying in* NOSTROMO*'s arms, speaking in a breathless whisper.*

GISELLE: Why have you done this terrible, cruel thing?

NOSTROMO: I was afraid I might lose you.

(*She kisses him as the beam passes over them, before being deflected up the front wall of the cottage.*)

GISELLE: Take me away from here. Now. Tonight.

NOSTROMO: Not yet.

GISELLE: Why not?

NOSTROMO: There is something which still stands between us.

GISELLE: What, my lover? What can there be?

(*He doesn't answer for a moment.*)

EXT. RAVINE. NIGHT

The cold light of the lighthouse beam passes across the beach and the ravine.

EXT. SIDE-WALL OF THE COTTAGE. NIGHT

NOSTROMO*'s eyes flash with a sudden excitement; he speaks impulsively.*

NOSTROMO: A treasure.

GISELLE: What?

NOSTROMO: I stole it. From the rich.

(GISELLE *is staring uncomprehendingly at* NOSTROMO.)

I was betrayed and I took my revenge. So you must give me two or three days. And then we will sail away and never return to this island. Or this country.

(GISELLE, *excited, presses herself against him, insisting.*)

GISELLE: Tonight, Gian' Battisa.

NOSTROMO: No. But soon. I will come for you soon. Like a thief.

(VIOLA*'s* VOICE *interrupts, calling out 'Giselle!' from inside the cottage.* GISELLE *sits up, brutally shocked. As she rises,* NOSTROMO *scrambles up, whispering urgently.*)

Tell him I didn't want to stay.

(*He slips away into the darkness.*)

EXT. WALLED GARDEN OF THE CASA GOULD. DAY

MRS GOULD *and* DR MONYGHAM *sit in wicker easy-chairs in the shade of an orange tree,* MONYGHAM *sipping his coffee. In the background, the gardeners are watering the lawn.*

MRS GOULD: So, what *is* the gossip?

MONYGHAM: I heard this morning that Nostromo has finally

put the question to the black-eyed Linda.

MRS GOULD: Only now? I'd expected to find them already married.

MONYGHAM: He's been too busy turning himself into a tycoon. He really has done extraordinarily well. And it's said he's now the principal financier of the various revolutionary groups trying to stir up trouble in the town.

MRS GOULD: I must speak to him about this. Hasn't there been enough trouble?

MONYGHAM: This is an incorrigible country.

(BASILIO, *now fat and sleek, approaches across the lawn.*)

MRS GOULD: What is it, Basilio?

BASILIO: A telephone call from the mine office. The master will be sleeping at the mountain tonight.

MRS GOULD: He'll be back for the dinner tomorrow?

BASILIO: They didn't say, Señora.

(*He turns and walks away as* MRS GOULD *tries to master her obvious disappointment.* MONYGHAM *watches, once again in the grip of the pleasures and pains he invariably feels in the presence of* MRS GOULD.)

MONYGHAM: And how did you enjoy your . . . grand tour?

MRS GOULD: Very much. (*She looks away for a moment, her melancholy expression belying her answer.*) Charley had a great deal of business to conduct, that goes without saying; he's always worked far too hard. Poor boy. What he needs is some rest, a little peace.

(MONYGHAM *shakes his head, sombre.*)

MONYGHAM: You should know by now: there is no peace and no rest in the development of material interests.

MRS GOULD: What do you mean?

MONYGHAM: Their demands have never been compatible with moral principles. Eventually, the Gould Concession will weigh as heavily on the people as any of the barbarities of the Civil War.

(MRS GOULD *shakes her head, genuinely appalled by his suggestion.*)

MRS GOULD: How can you say that?

MONYGHAM: I can say it because it's true.

MRS GOULD: But it's been the most colossal success. And

surely, to create something lasting, what could be more important than that?

MONYGHAM: Love, perhaps?

MRS GOULD: No. Love is only a moment of intoxication. Something you remember with sadness, like a bereavement.
(She breaks off, conscious of having revealed too much; and looks away, her eyes liquid. MONYGHAM *watches her, holding his breath, afraid to speak. She makes a great effort and turns back to him, speaking in her normal balanced tones.)*
Do you still dream about the priest?

MONYGHAM: No, I'm a changed man. *(He makes a gesture, indicating the silk handkerchief in his breast pocket and his impeccable dress-coat. Then he adds, in a scarcely audible murmur:)* Thanks to you, Emilia.
*(*MRS GOULD *looks at him, her expression tender. He scarcely dares to ask the next question.)*
What are you thinking?
(She looks at him for a moment, moved.)

MRS GOULD: No one but you has ever asked me that question and been genuinely interested in the reply.
(Their eyes meet; and they hold each other's gaze.)

INT. LAMP-ROOM. NIGHT

LINDA *stands in front of the revolving lamp, so that great aureoles of light stream out around her hair. She's staring out, unseeing, across the Gulf.*

EXT. BEACH. NIGHT

NOSTROMO *lowers his old leather satchel into the bottom of his dinghy. Then he turns and looks up towards* VIOLA*'s cottage.*

EXT. VIOLA'S COTTAGE. NIGHT

A light still burns in one of the windows.

INT. GISELLE'S BEDROOM. NIGHT

It's the GIRLS' *bedroom, where the light burns, a flickering candle between the two narrow beds.* GISELLE, *in her white nightdress, rises, prompted by some instinct.*

Her POV*: suddenly* NOSTROMO*'s face appears at the window.*

GISELLE *hurries to open the window. She leans out to kiss him, then speaks in a whisper.*

GISELLE: Have you come to take me away, my love?

NOSTROMO: Not yet. I told you. Soon.

(*He climbs easily into the room.* GISELLE *closes the window. They fall into each other's arms. The passing beam from the lighthouse silhouettes their tightly embracing figures against the window.*)

INT. GOULD'S QUARTERS INSIDE THE MINE. DAY

GOULD*'s quarters are a kind of gallery built inside the great cavern of the mine entrance, so arranged that he can look down on the activities below, see the ore arriving from the depths, loaded on to the wagons and conveyed towards the chutes.*

At present, he's engaged in a difficult conversation with MRS GOULD. *She looks very upset; and his demeanour is genuinely apologetic.*

GOULD: Just give everyone my apologies. I'm sure the Doctor will be happy to stand in for me.

MRS GOULD: I suppose it's always going to be like this.

GOULD: It's just that people have made mistakes in my absence: with the result that I find myself in the middle of an extremely complicated labour dispute.

MRS GOULD: But if it wasn't that, it would be something else.

GOULD: I'm afraid I have to do what's necessary, my dear.

MRS GOULD: That's the thing about success, I see it now: it brings with it certain necessities which cannot help but degrade one's original ideals.

GOULD: I don't think I can agree with that . . .

MRS GOULD: Oh, it's not your fault, none of this is your fault. But I begin to think your father was right, after all. It's just a different kind of curse. Perhaps it's lucky we were never able to have children.

(*For the first time,* GOULD *looks genuinely shocked.*)

GOULD: We agreed we were never going to speak of that.

MRS GOULD: I know: I'm sorry. It's only that I realize now I shall never have you to myself again. Not even for an hour.

GOULD: That's simply not true . . .

(*He breaks off as the door opens and* DON PEPE, *in a three-*

piece suit of antique cut, appears, hovering apologetically in the doorway. GOULD *is immediately himself again.*)
Ah, yes: I shall just take the señora to her carriage and then I'll join you.

INT. MINE ENTRANCE. DAY

GOULD *escorts* MRS GOULD *through the great space of the mine entrance, full of bustle and machinery, a cathedral of industry, towards the crash of the stamping-mills. A wagon loaded with ore trundles past her on its way to the chutes; she watches it for a moment, then turns back to* GOULD.

MRS GOULD: Material interests.
(*He doesn't quite know how to take this: and consequently doesn't answer.*)

EXT. MINE ENTRANCE. DAY

GOULD *helps his wife up into her carriage, which* IGNACIO *is driving. The sound of the stamping-mills is now deafening.* MRS GOULD *asks* GOULD *something. He shakes his head, unable to hear. She leans in towards him and repeats herself, shouting at the top of her lungs. He still can't hear and spreads his hands apologetically.* MRS GOULD *gives up and settles back in the carriage.*

GOULD *moves to the mine entrance, as* IGNACIO *gees up the horses. He turns silhouetted against the cavernous interior and waves to* MRS GOULD*: who, fighting back tears, waves back to him.*

INT. MINE ENTRANCE. DAY

GOULD *turns and sets off, back into the mine. The camera rests on his back, as he's gradually swallowed up into the darkness. Over this, the melancholy* VOICE *of* GOULD*'s* FATHER *returns.*

GOULD SR: (*Voice-over*) My boy, I don't suppose you remember the legend of the lost treasure of Azuera. Two sailors, *gringos* of some sort, went up into the mountains to search for some fabulous hoard.

EXT. ISLAND OF GREAT ISABEL. DAY

It's late afternoon and the sun has almost dipped below the horizon. NOSTROMO*'s dinghy has been pulled up on the little beach. The lighthouse towers above.*

GOULD SR: (*Voice-over*) They suffered a quite catastrophic fate. They found it.

EXT. RAVINE. DAY

NOSTROMO *has fitted as many ingots as he can into his satchel. He's nervous doing this by day, so he fumbles with the last ingot and then examines his hands, as if some tell-tale stain might have leaked from the silver. He rubs his hands against his trouser-legs, shuddering with distaste. Then he reaches for his spade and begins smoothing the ground.*

GOULD SR: (*Voice-over*) It fastened on them, wouldn't let them go. It wouldn't even let them die. They became the slaves of the treasure.

EXT. VIOLA'S COTTAGE. DAY

GISELLE, *sitting alone outside the cottage, looks up from her embroidery to see:*

NOSTROMO, *still some way off, who calls to her with a kind of artificial* bonhomie.

NOSTROMO: Giselle! Has Linda gone to the light?

GISELLE: Not yet.

(*She's answered in the same casual tone.* NOSTROMO *hurries to her side and his voice drops to a murmur.*)

NOSTROMO: I'll come to your window tonight.

GISELLE: No, don't. Linda knows.

NOSTROMO: What?

GISELLE: She knows.

NOSTROMO: How could she? Did you tell her?

GISELLE: No, of course not. But . . . I don't know . . . some instinct . . .

(*She breaks off, because* LINDA *has appeared in the doorway of the cottage with a bucket in her hand. She looks haggard and unhappy, with dark circles under her eyes.* NOSTROMO *hurries to her and enfolds her in a perfunctory embrace.*)

NOSTROMO: What's the matter? Are you ill?

(LINDA *looks up at him, her eyes burning feverishly. Then she breaks away and empties the bucket, flinging water across the grass in a violent gesture. Then she turns and vanishes back into the cottage, leaving* NOSTROMO *and* GISELLE *to eye one another guiltily.*)

EXT. VERANDAH IN THE CASA GOULD. NIGHT

MRS GOULD, *resplendently dressed for her dinner-party, beautiful in her silk dress, with its shimmering train, her diamond necklace dancing in the light, emerges from the Gran Sala on* DR MONYGHAM*'s arm and begins leading her guests in the direction of the dining-room.*

EXT. BEACH ON GREAT ISABEL. NIGHT

NOSTROMO *jumps out of his dinghy into the gentle surf and beaches it. The beam of the lighthouse passes overhead, in addition to which it's full moon. He reaches into the boat and jerks back a tarpaulin towards the stern. Underneath is an old wooden chest; and a spade which he fetches out of the boat.*

He advances a few paces up the beach and stops.

EXT. VIOLA'S COTTAGE. NIGHT

Once again, GISELLE*'s is the only light burning.*

EXT. BEACH. NIGHT

NOSTROMO *stares up at the light, tempted. Then he comes to a decision, turns, moves back to the dinghy and drops the spade back into the boat. He turns again, and sets off up the beach, a black shape against the sparkling sea. Suddenly, an unfamiliar sound stops him dead in his tracks: it's the click of a rifle bolt.*

VIOLA *steps from behind a tree, raises his rifle and fires.*

NOSTROMO, *hit in the chest, goes flying backwards on to the sand.*

The lighthouse beam passes over VIOLA: *his eyes are wide and staring.*

VIOLA*'s* POV*:* NOSTROMO *groans and writhes, his body black against the moonlit sand.*

VIOLA *frowns in recognition, lowering the rifle from his shoulder. Then he shakes his head, dismissing the idea the intruder might be* NOSTROMO.

EXT. LIGHTHOUSE. NIGHT

The lighthouse door is flung back. LINDA *steps out into the moonlight, looking wildly around her.*

EXT. BEACH. NIGHT

VIOLA *is still rooted to the spot, as* NOSTROMO *gasps with pain. Suddenly,* GISELLE *rushes down the hill, her nightdress streaming behind her, passes* VIOLA *and drops to her knees beside* NOSTROMO.

GISELLE: Gian' Battista!

(VIOLA*'s eyes narrow in puzzlement.*

A dark circle of blood stains NOSTROMO*'s white shirt.* GISELLE *takes his head in her hands and rests it on her thigh.*)

Why did you come? I told you not to come tonight. I told you.

(*She bursts into incoherent sobs.*

VIOLA *still hasn't moved. Now,* LINDA *arrives and stops next to him. She stands a moment, trying to take in what's happened.*

CLOSE *on* GISELLE *and* NOSTROMO.)

Why did you come?

(NOSTROMO *looks up at her, his eyes glittering, his voice weak.*)

NOSTROMO: I thought I couldn't live through the night without you.

(LINDA*'s face: she recoils, as if from a blow.* VIOLA *looks at her for a moment, still bewildered, before speaking in Italian.*)

VIOLA: The thief, Linda: why does he speak in Gian' Battista's voice?

(LINDA *looks at him without answering. Then she moves slowly away from him, down towards the beach. She stops a few feet away from* NOSTROMO *and* GISELLE. VIOLA *remains a black silhouette in the foreground.*

The beam of the lighthouse sweeps inexorably over the four of them.)

INT. GRAN SALA IN THE CASA GOULD. NIGHT

The party is over, most of the lights (which are now electric) are out: and MRS GOULD *sits, quite alone in the vast room, her mind altogether elsewhere. She looks up with a start, as* MONYGHAM *hobbles into the room.*

MRS GOULD: What is it, Doctor? Have you forgotten something?

MONYGHAM: There's been an accident. Nostromo has been hurt.

(MRS GOULD *has risen to her feet in alarm.*)

MRS GOULD: What kind of an accident?

MONYGHAM: I've had him brought here, he's downstairs in the patio. He's been asking to see you.

MRS GOULD: Me?

MONYGHAM: It seems there's something he wants to say to you.

EXT. PATIO IN THE CASA GOULD. NIGHT

NOSTROMO, *his chest tightly bandaged, lies on the top of* VIOLA*'s dining-table, the legs of which have been sawn off. He's in a corner of the patio, surrounded by a small knot of servants.* GISELLE *kneels beside him, trying unsuccessfully to control her sobs.*

MRS GOULD *comes down the stairs from the verandah, followed by* MONYGHAM, *the long train of her evening-dress rustling behind her.* NOSTROMO *watches them approach and speaks as they arrive at his side.*

NOSTROMO: Giselle.

GISELLE: Yes.

NOSTROMO: Go with the Doctor for a moment.

(*Reluctantly,* GISELLE *allows* MONYGHAM *to lead her away; as he does so, he shoos away the servants. He turns back to see:*

MRS GOULD, *indifferent to her gown, kneeling on the ground at* NOSTROMO*'s head.*)

MRS GOULD: How has this happened?

NOSTROMO: The old man thought he was shooting a thief.

(*His lips twist into an ironical smile.*)

And he was right.

MRS GOULD: What do you mean?

NOSTROMO: The consignment of silver your husband put in my charge . . .

MRS GOULD: Yes?

NOSTROMO: I stole it.

(*Silence, as* MRS GOULD *comes to terms with this information. Then, a thought strikes her.*)

MRS GOULD: And what became of Don Martin Decoud?

NOSTROMO: You think I killed him? No. He killed himself. And took four bars of silver with him. I don't know why. And now the silver has killed me.

(MRS GOULD *leans in very low and whispers in his ear.*)

MRS GOULD: I hate the silver too, Captain. From the bottom of my heart.

NOSTROMO: Wonderful luxury, to hate the wealth you people take from the hands of the poor.

(MRS GOULD *draws back, hurt; but* NOSTROMO *strains forward, anxious to unburden himself.*)

I asked for you to tell you where the silver is hidden.

MRS GOULD: No.

NOSTROMO: I chose you because you understand that wealth is a curse; and because you are like the silver. Incorruptible.

(MRS GOULD *lays a hand gently on his lips.*)

MRS GOULD: Please. Let it stay where it is. Let it be lost forever.

(*They look at each other for a long moment, the two victims of the silver. Then an enigmatic smile spreads across* NOSTROMO*'s face.* MRS GOULD *turns and beckons* DR MONYGHAM *and* GISELLE. *Still smiling,* NOSTROMO *reaches up for* GISELLE*'s hand. As she takes it, his head slumps to one side. He's dead.* GISELLE *bursts into racking sobs.* MONYGHAM *whispers to* MRS GOULD, *his voice alive with curiosity.*)

MONYGHAM: What was it he wanted to say to you? I've always felt there was some mystery about Nostromo. Did he . . . ?

MRS GOULD: He told me nothing.

(*She's interrupted with considerable brusqueness and he falls silent, afraid of having offended her. Meanwhile,* MRS GOULD *has concentrated her attention on* GISELLE, *whom she takes in her arms.*)

EXT. RAVINE ON GREAT ISABEL. DAWN

The ravine, the beach, the calm sea, in the first pearl-grey pre-dawn light. The moon is still huge in the sky. The beam from the lighthouse still revolves, illuminating, at it passes, the site of the lost treasure.

EXT. POLICE GALLEY. DAWN

NOSTROMO*'s body is laid out on a platform in the centre of the galley.* MRS GOULD, *now wearing a grey cloak with a hood, sits with* GISELLE *in her arms.* DR MONYGHAM *stands behind them. The oars rise and fall in the placid water.* GISELLE *is suddenly shaken with sobs and* MRS GOULD *draws her closer. A spasm of something almost like bitterness crosses her face.*

MRS GOULD: He would soon have forgotten you.

(GISELLE *stops crying, shocked.*)

GISELLE: Oh, no, signora. He loved me. He loved me.

MRS GOULD: I have been loved myself.

(MONYGHAM *is looking down at them, transfixed. And* GISELLE, *bewildered by the severity of* MRS GOULD*'s expression, begins to protest.*)

GISELLE: But you will always be loved and respected . . .

MRS GOULD: And as solitary as any human being on this earth.

EXT. LIGHTHOUSE. DAWN

A black figure is silhouetted against the glass of the lamp-room. Then LINDA *steps up to the rail of the metal balcony and a great cry goes ringing out across the waters of the Gulf.*

LINDA: Gian' Battista!

EXT. POLICE GALLEY. DAWN

DR MONYGHAM *looks up at the lighthouse as the last echoes of the cry die away. Then he catches* MRS GOULD*'s eye and they exchange a look of profound understanding. He lets a hand fall on her shoulder.*

MEDIUM SHOT *of the police-boat, as it glides out of frame.*

EXT. GOLFO PLACIDO. DAWN

A tinge of pink is beginning to appear on the horizon: but the surface of the Gulf is still raked by the powerful beam of the lighthouse. The sea is as flat and motionless as ever: and the screen is a sheet of silver.